HOW NOT TO DROWN

by Nicola McCartney and Dritan Kastrati

How Not To Drown was first performed on 4 August 2019 at the Traverse Theatre, Edinburgh.

‖SAMUEL FRENCH‖

samuelfrench.co.uk

FOR AMATEUR PRODUCTION ENQUIRIES

UNITED KINGDOM AND WORLD
EXCLUDING NORTH AMERICA
plays@samuelfrench.co.uk
020 7255 4302/01

Each title is subject to availability from Samuel French,
depending upon country of performance.

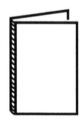

MUSIC USE NOTE

Licensees are solely responsible for obtaining formal written permission from copyright owners to use copyrighted music in the performance of this play and are strongly cautioned to do so. If no such permission is obtained by the licensee, then the licensee must use only original music that the licensee owns and controls. Licensees are solely responsible and liable for all music clearances and shall indemnify the copyright owners of the play(s) and their licensing agent, Samuel French, against any costs, expenses, losses and liabilities arising from the use of music by licensees. Please contact the appropriate music licensing authority in your territory for the rights to any incidental music.

USE OF COPYRIGHT MUSIC

A licence issued by Samuel French Ltd to perform this play does not include permission to use the incidental music specified in this copy.

Where the place of performance is already licensed by the PERFORMING RIGHT SOCIETY (PRS) a return of the music used must be made to them. If the place of performance is not so licensed then application should be made to the PRS, 2 Pancras Square, London, N1C 4AG. www.prsformusic.com

A separate and additional licence from PHONOGRAPHIC PERFORMANCE LTD, 1 Upper James Street, London W1F 9DE (www.ppluk.com) is needed whenever commercial recordings are used.

IMPORTANT BILLING AND CREDIT REQUIREMENTS

If you have obtained performance rights to this title, please refer to your licensing agreement for important billing and credit requirements.

AUTHORS' NOTE

What follows is a true story adapted and dramatised by Nicola McCartney from transcribed interviews conducted with Dritan Kastrati between 2014 and 2018, about his own life history. It follows a double survival story: of the epic journey he makes as an eleven-year-old asylum seeker, after the Kosovan war, when he must rely on his wits and his humour to get by; and then his battle to keep hold of his own identity and dignity as a non-English-speaking child refugee, voiceless and homeless, within the UK Care system.

Nicola McCartney & Dritan Kastrati
June 2019

How Not To Drown was first performed on 4 August 2019 at Traverse Theatre, Edinburgh with the following cast and creatives:

CAST

Dritan Kastrati
Ajjaz Awad
Esme Bayley
Daniel Cahill
Reuben Joseph

CREATIVES

Writers	Nicola McCartney & Dritan Kastrati
Direction & Choreography	Neil Bettles
Co-choreography	Jonnie Riordan
Design & Costume	Becky Minto
Composition & Sound Design	Alexandra Faye Braithwaite
Lighting	Zoe Spurr
Production Manager	Fiona Fraser
Stage Managers	Kara Jackson
	Jessica Ward
Production Electrician & Relighter	Andy Gannon
Set construction	Pretty Scenic & W A McGarrie & Son
Assistant Production Manager	Emma Campbell
Sound Associate	Annie May Fletcher
Executive Producer	Laura Mallows
Producer	Steph Connell
Associate Producer	Carla Marina Almeida
Publicist	SM Publicity

A ThickSkin and Traverse Theatre Company production, co-produced with Tron Theatre and Lawrence Batley Theatre. Commissioned by ThickSkin and Lawrence Batley Theatre.

Sponsored by Supper Club Compassion and supported by November Productions, Citizens Theatre and the National Lottery through Arts Council England and Creative Scotland. Part of Made in Scotland 2019.

Developed with support from The University of Edinburgh.

Nicola and Dritan would like to thank Albert Kastrati, Dritan's family, Scott Graham, Rosanna Hall, Inga Hirst, Jenny Knotts, Helene Groen, Jorida Ramadani and Wendy Timmons.

ThickSkin would also like to thank the Kastrati Family, Backstage Trust, City of Glasgow Council, Grid Iron, Royal Lyceum Theatre Edinburgh, National Theatre of Scotland, Royal Conservatoire of Scotland, Scottish Refugee Council, Leon Aarts, Andy Arnold, Caroline Boss, Daniel Cahill, Albi Cahini, Sokol Cahini, Professor Sharon Cowan, Linda Crooks, Lesley Davies, Caroline Donald, Henry Filloux-Bennett, Fiona Gregory, Alison Hargreaves, Steven Hoggett, Robbie Jack, Natali McCleary, Sharon McHendry, Itxaso Moreno, Sally Reid, Bruce Robertson, James Thompson and Adam Tompa.

ThickSkin dedicates this production to Derek Bettles.

CAST

DRITAN KASTRATI (CO-WRITER)

Dritan graduated from Frantic Assembly's Ignition Company in 2009, and was awarded a BBC Performing Arts Fund Bursary. He performed as Montano in Frantic's hit-show *Othello*. He has played the lead in the feature film *Pit Stop Mafia*, directed by Fatmir Koçi. He worked with Koçi again performing as Mickey in the 2016 feature film *Elvis Walks Home*, winning the Best Lead Actor at the International Film Festival Awards. Other recent acting credits: *Agatha Raison* Season 3 (Acorn Entertainment, 2019); *Stan Lee's Lucky Man* (Sky One, 2018); *All the Devil's Men* (Netflix, 2018); *Hooten & the Lady* (Sky, 2016) and *Houdini and Doyle* (Big Talk Productions, 2016).

How Not To Drown is the first play that he has written and is based on his true life story.

AJJAZ AWAD

Ajjaz Awad trained at RADA and ALRA. Recent theatre credits include: *The Hound Of The Baskerville* (The Mill at Sonning) and *Another Star To Steer By* (Brighton Dome). Television and radio credits include: *Holby City* and the radio series of *Dr. Who*. Director/Creative credits include: *Race Today* (Bernie Grant Arts Centre) and *good dog* (Tiata Fahodzi) and *Parrallel: Yerma* (The Young Vic). Ajjaz was the 2010 winner of The Lawrence Olivier Bursary. Ajjaz is also part of the Tamasha Theatre Company Writers Group 18/19, the Royal Court Writers Group 2019 and won the RTYDS Assistant Directors award 2017.

ESME BAYLEY

Esme trained at The University of Manchester and Royal Conservatoire of Scotland graduating with an MA Acting in Classical and Contemporary Text. Recent theatre credits include: *Gaslight* (Perth Theatre at Horsecross Arts); *Edward the Second, Romeo & Juliet, Measure for Measure, Taming of the Shrew* (Bard in the Botanics); *Ricky McWhittington* (Glasgow Life); *Look Back in Anger* (Cumbernauld Theatre) and *Secret Show 1* (Blood of the Young / Tron Theatre).

DANIEL CAHILL

Daniel trained at the Royal Conservatoire of Scotland. Theatre credits include: *All My Sons* (Dundee Rep); *The First Dance* (Oran Mor); *Macbeth* (Stafford Gatehouse Theatre); *Shift* (National Theatre of Scotland); *Small World* (National Theatre of Scotland); *James I, James II* and *James III* (National Theatre / National Theatre of Scotland);

Lot and His God (Citizens Theatre); *Truant* (National Theatre of Scotland) and *Blackout* (ThickSkin). TV/Film credits include: *Cassette* (Parkhouse Pictures); *Pumped* (BBC3); *Anna and the Apocalypse* (Blazing Griffin); *Blackout* (Oscar Films); *Exodus 21:24* (Blazing Griffin); *Outpost 3: Rise of the Spetsnaz* (Cinema 3) and *River City* (BBC Scotland). Director/Creative credits include: *Jump, Run Free* in Jamaica and *Jump!* in Trinidad and Tobago (National Theatre of Scotland); *Rock, White Noise* and *Bring Your Own* (ThickSkin).

REUBEN JOSEPH

Reuben trained at Glasgow Clyde College and graduated in 2018. Theatre credits include: *The Cheviot, the Stag and the Black, Black Oil* and *Midsummer* (National Theatre Scotland); *Anything That Gives Off Light* (The TEAM); *A Christmas Carol* (Citizens Theatre); *Arsenic and Old Lace, The Hobbit, Animal Farm, The Day the Whores Came Out to Play Tennis, Picnic at Hanging Rock* (Glasgow Clyde College); *We're Here Because We're Here* (National Theatre Scotland / NOW 14-18); *The Island* (Platform Young Company) and *The History Boys* (Glasgow Acting Academy).

CREATIVES

NICOLA MCCARTNEY - WRITER

Nicola McCartney is a playwright, director and dramaturg. She trained as a director with Citizen Theatre/G&J Productions and Charabanc Theatre Company, Belfast. Nicola was Artistic Director of Lookout Theatre Company, Glasgow from 1992–2002, and has twice been an Associate Playwright of Playwrights' Studio Scotland. She has worked for a host of organisations as a dramaturg including Vanishing Point and Stellar Quines/Edinburgh International Festival. Her plays include: *Easy, Heritage, Home, Standing Wave: Delia Derbyshire in the 60s, Rachel's House, Cave Dwellers* and *Lifeboat*. She is also a social theatre practitioner and has worked with all sorts of groups including people within the criminal justice system in the UK and USA, asylum seekers and refugees, drug users, survivors of domestic violence and childhood abuse. Nicola has worked with Traverse's flagship outreach programme, Class Act, since 1997, taking it to Russia, Ukraine and India. In 2018 she was a recipient of a Writers' Guild of Great Britain Olwen Wymark Award for encouraging theatre in the UK. Nicola is currently Reader in Writing for Performance at the University of Edinburgh where she leads the Masters programme in Playwriting.

NEIL BETTLES - DIRECTOR

Neil is co-founder and Artistic Director of ThickSkin, where his directing credits include: *Chalk Farm, The Static* and *Blackout* and as co-director: *Boy Magnet* and *White Noise* for the company. He is Associate Director for Frantic Assembly recently directing *The Unreturning* (UK Tour) and *This Will All Be Gone* (International Tour), he co-directed *No Way Back* (Corby Cube) and was Assistant Director of *Dirty Wonderland* (Brighton Festival). Neil is International Associate Movement Director on *Harry Potter And The Cursed Child* having worked on the West End, Broadway and Melbourne productions. Other credits include: Associate Director of *We Are Here* (La Mama, New York). As Movement Director: *Carmen* (Opera Wuppertal, Germany); *The James Plays* (Edinburgh International Festival and National Theatre); *Blood Wedding* and *The Bacchae* (Royal & Derngate). As Associate Movement Director: *Heisenberg* (Wyndhams Theatre); *The Light Princess* (National Theatre) and *The Full Monty* (Sheffield Theatres and West End). www.neilbettles.co.uk

JONNIE RIORDAN - CO-CHOREOGRAPHER

Jonnie is ThickSkin's Associate Director. Recent theatre directing credits include: *AWOL* and *Boy Magnet* (ThickSkin) and *Nigel Slater's Toast* (West End). As Movement Director: *Great Apes* (Arcola Theatre); *Maggie & Pierre* (Finborough Theatre); *Mobile* (Paper Birds) and

Home (Frozen Light). As an actor, he has appeared in *The Unreturning* (Frantic Assembly, UK tour); *This Will All Be Gone* (Frantic Assembly); *No Way Back* (Frantic Assembly/Made in Corby); *Full Stop* (Light The Fuse/Lyric Hammersmith/Greenwich and Docklands International Festival); *Canticles* (Brighton Festival/Aldeburgh Music/Frantic Assembly). www.jonnieriordan.co.uk

BECKY MINTO - DESIGNER

Becky has designed over 100 productions for main-house and touring theatre productions, aerial and dance performances, site-specific and large outdoor events across Scotland the UK and Europe. *The 306: Dawn* (National Theatre of Scotland) won the Silver Medal for Space Design at World Stage Design Exhibition 2017. Her work was selected to represent the UK at the Staging Places Exhibition at the Prague Quadrennial and the V&A London in 2019 and 2015. She was Associate Designer for the Opening and Designer for the Closing Ceremonies of the Glasgow 2014 Commonwealth Games. Recent designs include: *Ulster American* (Traverse Theatre); *Catch Me* (Upswing); *Flight Paths* (Extant/Yellow Earth) and *The Ugly One* (Tron Theatre). Upcoming projects include: *Frankenstein* (Perth Rep) and *Hope and Joy* (Pearlfisher).

ALEXANDRA FAYE BRAITHWAITE - SOUND DESIGNER & COMPOSER

Alex's recent theatre credits include: *Enough* (Traverse Theatre), *Nigel Slater's Toast* (West End), *Hamlet, Talking Heads, Rudolf* (Leeds Playhouse); *Cougar, Dealing With Clair, The Rolling Stone* (Orange Tree Theatre); *Romeo And Juliet* (China Plate); *My Name Is Rachel Corrie* (The Faction); *Things of Dry Hours* (Young Vic); *Acceptance* (Hampstead Theatre); *Chicken Soup* (Sheffield Crucible); *Dublin Carol* (The Sherman); *Room* (Stratford East/The Abbey); *If I Was Queen* (The Almeida); *The Remains of Maisie Duggan* (The Abbey); *Happy To Help* (Park Theatre); *The Tempest* (Royal & Derngate); *The Future* (The Yard); *The Audience, Juicy & Delicious* (Nuffield Theatre), *Dairy of a Madman* (Gate Theatre/ Traverse). Upcoming projects include: *Light Falls* and *Wuthering Heights* (Manchester Royal Exchange) and *Groan Ups* (The Vaudeville). www.alexandrafayebraithwaite.com

ZOE SPURR - LIGHTING DESIGNER

Zoe trained at Royal Central School of Speech and Drama. Recent theatre includes: *Onegin, Georgiana* and *Lucio Papirio Dittatore* (Buxton International Festival / Buxton Opera House); *Emilia* (Vaudeville Theatre); *The Phlebotomist* (Hampstead Theatre); *The Maids* (HOME Manchester); *Cat In The Hat* (Leicester Curve / UK Tour); *The Unreturning* (Frantic Assembly / UK Tour); *Nigel Slater's*

Toast (The Other Palace, Traverse 1); *Meek* (Headlong / UK Tour); *Abigail's Party* (Queens Theatre Hornchurch); *Confidence, Natives, Collective Rage* (Southwark Playhouse); *Tiny Dynamite* (Old Red Lion); *Phoenix Rising, Loose Lips* (Big House Theatre Company); *The Beginners* (Unicorn Theatre); *Elephant* (Birmingham REP); *The Magic Flute* (Soho Theatre / UK tour) and *Good Dog* (Watford Palace / UK Tour). www.zoespurrlighting.co.uk

FIONA FRASER - PRODUCTION MANAGER

Fi is the Production Manager for Imaginates' Edinburgh International Children's Festival. She has Production Managed over 22 productions for Grid Iron and headed the Stage Management team who won the 2004 SMA (Stage Management Association) excellence in Stage Management Award. She's production managed for Vanishing Point since 2009. Managing all national and international tours of *Interiors, Saturday Night, Wonderland, The Beautiful Cosmos of Ivor Cutler, Tomorrow, The Destroyed Room, Tabula Rasa* and most recently *The Dark Carnival*. She recently set up a company, Fi Fraser Production Management with the aim to work with and mentor emerging Production Managers. This is her second time working with ThickSkin. www.fifraser.com

JESSICA WARD - STAGE MANAGER

Jessica studied at Manchester Metropolitan University graduating with BA hons in Contemporary Theatre and Performance before training at Edinburgh Lighting and Sound School. Recent theatre credits: *Lost at Sea, Miss Julie, Snow White and the Seven Dames* (Perth Theatre); *306: Dusk* (Perth Theatre And National Theatre of Scotland); *Ulster American* and *Swallow* (Traverse Theatre); *The Whip Hand* (Traverse Theatre and Birmingham Rep); *Rhinoceros, Charlie Sonata* and *The Weir* (Lyceum Theatre) and *Wind Resistance* (Lyceum Theatre and Karine Polwart).

KARA JACKSON - STAGE MANAGER

Kara graduated from Queen Margaret University with a BA in Theatre Production specialising in Stage Management. She has worked with National Theatre of Scotland, Pachamama/Richard Jordan, Theatre503, Trafalgar Studios, Paines Plough, Oran Mor, Random Accomplice, Barrowland Ballet, RCS, Scottish Opera, Grid Iron, Stellar Quines, Imaginate, Lung Ha's, Traverse Theatre and works extensively both nationally and internationally with Vanishing Point.

ANDREW GANNON - PRODUCTION ELECTRICIAN

Andrew is a freelance Theatre Technician and Lighting Designer. Andrew has worked and toured with many companies including Vanishing Point (*Interiors, Tomorrow, The Dark Carnival*); Tortoise in a Nutshell (*Fisk, Feral*) and the National Theatre of Scotland (*Eve*). He has also designed lighting for Grid Iron, Lung Ha's Theatre Company and Tortoise in Nutshell. Andrew was Technical Manager at Edinburgh International Children's Festival 2019.

LAURA MALLOWS - EXECUTIVE PRODUCER

Laura Mallows is co-founder of ThickSkin. For ThickSkin she has Executive Produced: *Chalk Farm, The Static, Blackout, White Noise* and *Boy Magnet*, and designed the concept for *Matchbox Productions*. She also works as an independent arts consultant and producer. Laura was previously Head of Finance & Business at Clean Break. Laura was Associate Producer on *Beautiful Burnout* (Frantic Assembly / National Theatre of Scotland) and supported Frantic Assembly's productions of *Pool (no water), Stockholm* and *Othello* in the role of General Manager, and instigated the company's celebrated Ignition training programme. She has also worked with Fifty Nine Productions, Hofesh Schechter Company, Manchester International Festival, Royal Opera House, Shobana Jeyasingh Dance, The Cholmondeleys and The Featherstonehaughs, and Touring Consortium. www.lauramallows.co.uk

STEPH CONNELL - PRODUCER

ThickSkin's Producer, credits include: *AWOL* and *Chalk Farm* (UK and International Tour) and as Assistant Producer: *The Static* (International Tour). She is also Producer for Wonder Fools recently producing *549: Scots of the Spanish Civil War*. Steph was Stage One Producer at the Citizens Theatre in 2017. Other producing credits include: *No Way Back* (Frantic Assembly); *Leaper – A Fish Tale* and *Finding Victoria* (Tucked In); *Full Stop* (Light The Fuse/ Scribbled Thought); *Playground Victories* (Light The Fuse / Scribbled Thought) and *Superhero Snail Boy* (Scribbled Thought). Steph has also worked for Artichoke, National Theatre of Scotland, Greenwich and Docklands International Festival, National Centre for Circus Arts and is currently Project Coordinator at the Tron Theatre. www.stephconnell.co.uk

CARLA MARINA ALMEIDA - ASSOCIATE PRODUCER

Carla has an MA in Creative and Cultural Entrepreneurship from Goldsmiths. She is a freelance Producer, Performance Programmer for Paisley Arts Centre and Coordinator for Sofar Sounds Glasgow. She has also worked for Dundee Rep, Wilton's Music Hall and National Theatre's River Stage Festival. Recent credits include: Rep Stripped Festival and *Gagarin Way* (Dundee Rep); *Drowning* (Curve Theatre, Stockholm and UK wide); *Blackout* (Vault Festival); *Agent of Influence: The Secret Life of Pamela More* (Theatre503, Underbelly Edinburgh).

ThickSkin

'all the ingredients to inspire a new generation in theatre'
The Good Review

ThickSkin creates innovative and exciting theatre. The company was formed by Neil Bettles and Laura Mallows in 2010 and quickly established itself as one of the UK's most exciting theatre companies, producing award-winning productions, commissioning new writing and touring worldwide.

We aim to unearth new talent and engage established artists in the creation of new work. We nurture and enable them to take risks and test new ways of working. Our productions provide critical exposure and a springboard for artists ready to take a leap. In doing so we support the sector by finding, commissioning and showcasing diverse talent.

We hope to reach and inspire audiences through our distinctive physicality and cinematic style. The company is based in Manchester and Glasgow and makes work across the UK.

Artistic Director	Neil Bettles
Executive Director	Laura Mallows
Associate Director	Jonnie Riordan
Producer	Steph Connell
Associate Producer	Carla Marina Almeida
Supported Artists	groupwork
	Luke Brown Dance

thickskintheatre.co.uk

 @ThickSkinTweets

 /ThickSkinTheatre

 CREATIVE SCOT LAND   ALBA | CHRUTHACHAIL

 Supported using public funding by ARTS COUNCIL ENGLAND

BackstageTrust

ABOUT TRAVERSE THEATRE

As Scotland's new writing theatre, the Traverse Theatre is a dynamic centre for performance, experience and discovery, often referred to as Edinburgh's 'beating heart of the Fringe' in August. Enabling people across society to access and engage with theatre is our fundamental mission.

Our year-round programme bursts with new stories and live performances that challenge, inform and entertain. We empower artists and audiences to make sense of the world today, providing a safe space to question, learn, empathise and – crucially – encounter different people and experiences. Conversation and the coming together of groups are central to a democratic society, and we champion equal expression and understanding.

We commission, produce and programme for existing and future audiences to offer new and exciting experiences for everyone, and our partnerships with other theatre companies and festivals enable us to present a wide range of innovative performances.

The Traverse would not exist without our over-arching passion for talent development and embracing the unexplored. We work with the newest and rawest talent – with an emphasis on the Scottish-based – nurturing it to become the art, artists and performances that can be seen on our stages through a variety of creative learning and literary programmes.

The timely, powerful stories that start life on our stages have global impact, resulting in dozens of tours, productions and translations. We are critically acclaimed and recognised the world over for our originality and artistic risk, which we hope will create some of the most talked-about plays, productions, directors, writers and actors for years to come.

Find out more about the Traverse: traverse.co.uk

The Traverse Theatre extends grateful thanks to all those who generously support our work, including those who prefer their support to remain anonymous.

TRAVERSE THEATRE SUPPORTERS
Diamond   Alan and Penny Barr, Katie Bradford, Kirsten Lamb, David Rodgers
Platinum   Angus McLeod, Iain Millar
Gold   Carola Bronte-Stewart
Silver   Bridget M. Stevens, Allan Wilson, Judy & Steve
Bronze   Barbara Cartwright, Alex Oliver & Duncan Stephen

TRUSTS, FOUNDATIONS AND GRANTS
Anderson Anderson & Brown Charitable Initiative
Backstage Trust
British Council: UK/India 2017 Fund
British Council Scotland and Creative Scotland: UK in Japan 2019-20
The Cross Trust
Dr David Summers Charitable Trust
The Fidelio Charitable Trust

LAWRENCE BATLEY
THEATRE
HUDDERSFIELD

1994 *Celebrating 25 years* 2019

Over the last 25 years the Lawrence Batley Theatre has played host to some of the UK's most amazing, entertaining and ambitious companies, but we have never forgotten where we come from: we're a theatre created *by* the community in a building created *for* the community.

We present the very best touring drama, dance, circus, comedy and live music, and we produce and commission work for our three spaces as well, but we couldn't do what we do without the incredible support of our audiences and our two major funders...all of whom we're profoundly grateful to.

Supported using public funding by
ARTS COUNCIL ENGLAND

Kirklees COUNCIL

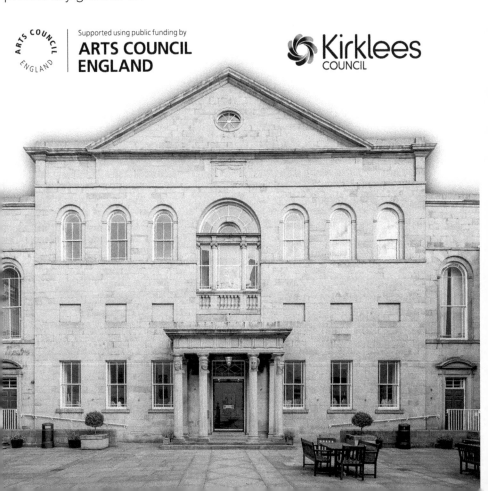

Find us. Tag us. Tweet us.

 /thelbt.org

 @lawrencebatleytheatre

 @theLBT

Find out more about the Lawrence Batley Theatre and what's on this season at **thelbt.org**

The team working at the Lawrence Batley Theatre is made up of Adele Barclay, Annie Baskeyfield-Bride, Adele Birkenshaw, Tom Blakemore, Freyja Boycott-Garnett, Chris Brearley, Paul Caldwell, James Clare, Craige Clarke, Holly Czolacz, Will Dash, Les Dowie, George Doyle, Karl Eaton, Henry Filloux-Bennett, Sarah Finch, Leah Fisher, Jenny Goodman, Andrew Goulding, Jack Greening, Bev Haigh, Sharon Haigh, David Halloran, Jonathan Hudson, Nancy Hughes , Ruth Jones, Connor Moseley, John Munden, Amy Norman, Laura Norman, Mass Nying, Judy O'Brien, Louise Parsons, Helen Petty, Cathy Pilkington, Olivia Race, Louise Redfearn, Jaqueline Ryan, Roohi Sarwar, Tommy Savage, Jane Sibbald, Jessica Smith, Brett Speakman, Ellie Stringer, Erica Taylor, Le Thi To Nhu, Rebecca Turner, Tom Walsh, Katherine Warman, Dianne Watkinson, Che Wigfield-Turner, Rebecca Winwood, Keren Wood, Mollie Wood and James Yates-Hothersall.

TRON THEATRE

The Tron Theatre Company is currently under the artistic leadership of Andy Arnold, who took up the position of Artistic Director and Chief Executive in 2008. The Tron Theatre presents the people of Glasgow and the West of Scotland with outstanding professional productions of the finest new writing, with an emphasis on world, UK and Scottish premieres; as well as staging co-productions and collaborations with other theatre companies and supporting the work of new and emergent artists.

Facebook /trontheatre
Twitter @trontheatre
Instagram @trontheatre

GRANT FUNDERS
Creative Scotland
Glasgow City Council
Glasgow Community Planning Partnership

SPONSORS
Arts and Business Scotland
Bellhaven

CORPORATE PARTNERS
ALBA Facilities Services
GH Digital Print
Alliance Wine
Belle and Blackley Hair and Beauty
Integro
Jamhot
Mercure Hotels

TRUSTS & FOUNDATIONS
Backstage Trust
Cruden Foundation
Jennie S Gordon Memorial Foundation
Miss E C Hendry Charitable Trust
PF Charitable Trust
Raymond Kenneth Thomas Harris Charitable Trust
SUEZ Communities Trust
The Cattanach Trust
The D'Oyly Carte Charitable Trust

The Hugh Fraser Foundation
The JTH Charitable Trust
The Merchants House of Glasgow
The Robert Barr Charitable Trust
The W M Mann Foundation
The W.A. Cargill Fund
Theatres Trust
Trades House of Glasgow
The Robert Haldane Smith Charitable Foundation
Bellahouston Bequest Fund
Garfield Weston Foundation
Mr and Mrs William Donalds Memorial Trust
The James Wood Bequest Fund
Mickel Fund
Foyle Foundation
Tesco - Bags of Help
John Mather Trust
The Allan & Nesta Ferguson Charitable Settlement
Ernest Cook Trust
WCH Trust for Children
The Endrick Trust
The Wolfson Foundation
Garrick Charitable Trust
The Swire Charitable Trust
Chance to Flourish – Scotland's Children's Lottery

STAFF
Box Office and Front of House Manager	Khaliq Ahmed
Artistic Director	Andy Arnold
Cleaner	Daniela Balogova
Finance Manager	Kate Bell
Early Years Outreach Coordinator	Victoria Bianchi
Creative Learning Manager (Maternity Cover)	Julie Brown

BESA

"If you can help someone, then why not?"

CHARACTERS

A Chorus of actors who play all the parts, sometimes including Dritan himself; a cast of 5 or 6 max.

DRITAN – a Kosovan-Albanian refugee; various ages 6–28 yrs, played by Dritan and the Chorus

DAD – Ibish

MUM – Bute

ALFRED – Dritan's older brother

LULI – Dritan's eldest sister

TILA – Dritan's second eldest sister

RICKY

GENZI

ANDI – Dritan's loyal childhood friend

THE BIG BOSS

JIMMY

TRAIN TICKET INSPECTOR

PARISIAN TICKET SALESPERSON

FOSTER CARERS – Indian parents, Sandra and Bill, Geoffrey and Anne, John and Gillian, Mary and Brian

STEPHEN – Sandra & Bill's son

ENVER – another Albanian kid in care

GARETH – another kid in care

ALEX – another kid in care with Dritan

DAVE – Dritan's school friend

PRISCILLA – a social worker (South African)

MICHAEL TULLOCH – a teacher

VARIOUS:

ALFRED'S GANG

DRITAN'S GANG

REFUGEES FROM ACROSS THE BORDER

OTHER REFUGEES, KURDS, KOSOVANS, ALBANIANS; ETC

GANGSTERS/MAFIA DUDES – various

POLICE

EXOTIC DANCERS – in Brussells strip club

MEN IN BAR

IMMIGRATION OFFICER

SOCIAL WORKERS

TRANSLATORS

SCHOOL KIDS

SETTING

A journey through Eastern and mainland Europe to the UK before and after the Kosovan War.

A note on production and casting

This script was written to be performed as a piece of physical theatre for an ensemble cast. The original ensemble casting included Dritan Kastrati himself.

Dritan, as a child, before he leaves home 2001.

Prologue: Learning to Swim

A river. DRITAN *and some other* BOYS *messing about in and by the water.*

DRITAN/CHORUS I think they chucked me in cos I was a little shit. And because, well, you have to learn, don't you? I was six years old. They'd always told me they would try.

ALFRED One day, we're gonna teach you how to swim.

DRITAN/CHORUS I just didn't know when. At that moment I was too relaxed. It was a nice day. I'm loving it...

There was two places we'd go swimming. But the first time I got chucked in was the river. My brother Alfred and his mates, they'd dive from the top of the waterfall right into it, but I would never do that, or go by myself in the river... Whoah...

Everyone had their little gang – all the boys. Alfred was six years older than me.

ALFRED Hey, little shit. Come on.

DRITAN/CHORUS So, this day, his gang are diving off the top of the waterfall, and I was just throwing stones at them, and hitting them. And because they was diving, there was nothing they could do about it. Just a little shit. And they thought

ALFRED'S GANG – Fuck you, come on then.

– We always told you we'd teach you to swim.

They throw DRITAN *into the river. He sinks under water.*

DRITAN/CHORUS It's cold

Whoah

Panic panic panic panic

And just

Go go go

DRITAN *starts drowning and fighting it.*

Forward Forward Forward

Or down

No

He swims.

Forward forward

Until my feet touch the floor

And now I'm on the other side of the river

The **BOYS** *on the other side of the river laugh in his face.*

And I'm like cry-laughing

"Fucking bastards!"

ALFRED'S GANG – Come on.

   – Come back

   – You can do it.

   – Tan!

THE REAL DRITAN That's me by the way: I am Tan: Dritan.

CHORUS I am Dritan.

I'm Dritan.

I am Dritan.

I'm Dritan.

THE REAL DRITAN But I'm the real deal. Anyway, this story you are about to see really happened. To me.

DRITAN/CHORUS "Fuck you! No!"

No way am I getting back in that water. Not today. How am I getting back home? Getting back? I had to go the long way around. Finally, I find some stepping stones and –

He crosses the river on stepping stones.

ALFRED Hahaha where've you been?

DRITAN/CHORUS My brother Alfred and his mates. Bigger shits.

1. The War in Kosova

DAD Alfred was always business-minded. From the age of fourteen, buying cigarettes, alcohol, and going backwards and forwards across the border between Kosova and Albania and selling it. For triple the price. Trying to make money. Cos he wanted to leave. He always wanted to leave.

DRITAN/CHORUS Why, Dad?

DAD Because there is no money. The government have spent it all. And there are no jobs.

(suddenly there are guns everywhere) And there are guns everywhere.

MUM Everyone has a gun now. At least one.

DAD Because there are wars in the Balkans.

War, chaos and confusion.: death, torture, people grabbing possessions, fleeing, crossing borders.

MUM War is everywhere: Bosnia, Croatia, Slovenia... And now Kosova.

DRITAN Why, Marmi?

DAD When was there not a war in our countries? There have been wars for six hundred years in our countries. And now there is another one.

MUM Because there is no Communism anymore. Because all the peoples want their freedom.

DAD At the expense of another people's freedom. And now Milosevic has pushed Albanians in Kosova too far. He is massacring our people and now Albanians everywhere are rising up.

DRITAN I don't understand.

MUM Serbians control what is left of Yugoslavia and they want to keep Kosova a part of it. It was never theirs to own.

DRITAN/CHORUS We live in the mountains near the border.

Between Kosova and Albania.

I can practically see the border from my house.

But I've never looked at it properly before.

MUM There is no border between Kosovans and Albanians. We are the same people. With the same language, the same flag and the same heart.

DAD Once Kosova was part of Albania. We were united, the same country.

MUM For six hundred years Kosova has had shifting borders. Like the tide going in and out.

DRITAN Why?

MUM Because it's right in the middle of Europe, halfway between East and West, North and South.

DAD And there's lots of gold mines. Lots. It's rich, so everyone wants a piece of it.

MUM And every time the tide goes in and out, people have to flee their homes.

DRITAN/CHORUS Where I live is a place called Has. And across the border there is a place called Has. A Has in Albania, and a Has in Kosova.

MUM There are a lot of places like that in Kosova and Albania, with the same name. And we are the same people, cut in two.

DAD After World War Two, the Allies carved up all our countries yet again, and Kosova was given to Yugoslavia.

MUM And now Yugoslavia is dying and there are so many wars all over the Balkans.

DAD And now in Kosova, the Serbians are driving out the Kosovan-Albanians.

MUM Driving them into their graves, you mean.

DRITAN I think I understand that.

DRITAN/CHORUS And that war...

Is getting closer

Closer

Closer

A stream of refugees.

I wake up one morning and in my village is just...people.
Thousands. Fleeing the bloodshed.

A family stays with us – parents and two kids older than me
and my brother. They came from a city called Gjakova, an
ancient city, a beautiful city, a wealthy city, but now totally
flattened and burned to the ground. Except the Serbian
people's houses – they had been left untouched. This family
are really wealthy, but they come to us on foot with nothing,
just the clothes on their backs. They stayed with us cos my
dad said:

DAD If you can do something for someone, then, why not? If
I can help them I should help them.

DRITAN/CHORUS Besa: "word of honour". That's how my Dad
was. Is. And that's how it is in my culture. Everyone else
in our village has people, family, staying with them too.

CHORUS – There's too many people coming into our village /
and the villages near us.

– We can't cope.

– How do we feed / everybody?

– We'll feed them. / No problem.

– How do we / house everybody?

– Here, who /needs blankets?

– Move on. / Move south.

– The war is getting closer.

– You can stay here. / Of course.

– We have / to move south.

– The Albanian government's / getting scared that Serbia might invade Albania.

– They don't want the people to get / caught like sheep and us all...just get killed.

– The war is getting closer and closer.

– Who needs clothes? / I have clothes here.

– The Serbians are going / to kill all Albanians.

– They won't stop til every one of us is dead, I swear it.

DRITAN/CHORUS Sometimes I hear gunfire.

CHORUS – The Serbian army are shooting animals/ in the fields.

   – The Serbs are burning down / all the mosques.

   – They are building churches / everywhere.

   – Since when was there / so many churches in Kosova?

   – The army surrounded our village, / then the police they came in.

   – They pulled children / out of the schools.

   – They beat old men / in the street.

   – In Gjakova they hung people / on gallows all along both sides of the main road.

   – They are raping pregnant women / and cutting their bellies open.

   – They rape women in front of their husbands / and children and then they kill the whole family.

   – I saw it myself.

DRITAN/CHORUS Sometimes I think I can hear screaming.

   Fire. Destruction. Terror.

CHORUS They will not stop until we are all dead.

DRITAN/CHORUS What if that happens here...?

   What if that happens to my family?

After the war ended, I remember going back down into Kosova with my dad, just to have a look. And everything was burned. As we drove through the mountains, I could smell...this stink. There were herds of dead animals but that was a different smell. I just knew that the stink was... dead bodies... And on the way down there were lots of open pits by the roadside, filled up with the dead, piled on top of each other. Burned, shot, cut open.

I was nine years old.

When you are little though, you just think, "Oh."

I didn't really register it, you know...the terror.

2. Training and Testing

DAD *sets* DRITAN *physical tests, running, jumping, throwing, climbing.*

DRITAN/CHORUS Looking back now, before I left home, when I was a little kid, it was like my dad was testing me.

DAD Training you.

DRITAN/CHORUS My mum worked a lot. So I didn't see her much.

MUM I'm a pharmacist. That's what I do. Medicines and stuff. There aren't many of us in the mountains and so that means I have to travel a lot. But don't worry. Your Dad will look after you.

DRITAN/CHORUS My dad worked too but I was with him most of the time.

DAD Dritan. Come on.

DRITAN/CHORUS Everything was me and him. I feel really lucky because a lot of the training my Dad used to sneak in gradually as a joke or whatever.

DAD I'm giving you... It's like a toolkit. And you'll always have that.

DRITAN/CHORUS Like with money. Like with thieving and stuff.

DAD I leave money somewhere, a little change under the bed, pretend I've dropped it.

DRITAN/CHORUS Or he had this safe where he'd keep all his money and sometimes...

DAD I leave the safe open.

DRITAN/CHORUS When he knew I was the only one in the house.

DAD And then I leave... You never ever touch the money.

DRITAN/CHORUS I would never touch the money. I would know that the money is there but unless he said, "take it..."

DAD Then I come back and check to see if the money is still there.

DRITAN/CHORUS He was testing me.

DAD To see what kind of man you will be. To see if you'd do something that isn't right.

DRITAN/CHORUS Training me.

DAD Instead of telling you not to touch this money, I am asking you, "Would you do it?"

DRITAN/CHORUS At school I was quite short.

DAD But relentless.

DRITAN/CHORUS And I always wanted to know about guns.

DAD If anyone leaves a gun down you're straight at it. Pick it up.

DRITAN/CHORUS It was fascinating.

DAD Too fascinating.

DRITAN/CHORUS It was a machine gun. An AK-47. My Dad allowed me to do it. I was so small I couldn't actually load the rifle because it was bigger than me. But I lay on the floor and loaded it with my feet.

DAD It's okay. Don't worry. Try to hit the same strip of dirt at least five times.

> **DAD** *covers* **DRITAN**'s *ears.*

DRITAN No, I wanna hear it.

> *He fires.*

DRITAN/CHORUS So I knew how to use it and not be scared of it. But I also wouldn't touch it alone.

Dad, why do you have a gun?

DAD Everyone needs a gun, Dritan.

DRITAN/CHORUS I loved the sound.

> *Some shady guys enter.*

DRITAN/CHORUS There was another time he tested me which I think now was a little bit dangerous. He put a fake bullet in the front of the magazine, so I'd assume it was full and left the gun and the magazine out...

DAD I want to see what you would do if...

DRITAN/CHORUS If what...?

The guys attack his DAD and rob him. DRITAN gets the gun and put the magazine in with his feet.

I am only six years old.

DRITAN points the gun at the older guys.

DRITAN You let my dad go. Now.

DRITAN/CHORUS *(to audience)* What would you do in that situation?

I try to fire the gun.

Nothing.

I try again.

And again.

And Dad says:

DAD Dritan. The clip is empty.

They all start laughing.

It's okay. This isn't real. These are my friends. I asked them to pretend to do it. I wanted to see what you would do.

DRITAN/CHORUS I was so angry that he had done this to me, that he was laughing at me.

DAD I'm not laughing at you... Dritan... Stop. Listen to me. I am serious. Now you know where the gun is. And where the bullets are... And I know what you will do if this happens for real next time. Do you understand?

DRITAN I understand.

3. Alfred Leaves

DRITAN/CHORUS I found out about Alfred leaving. I saw him go. He was always talking about it with his friends –

ALFRED I wanna leave. I'm getting out of here, soon as I get enough money.

ALFRED'S MATES – Where are you going to go?

– Where will you get the money from?

ALFRED I'm getting the money. I'm sorting it.

DRITAN/CHORUS To me, I was only little, it was like he was going on this adventure. I didn't know that meant away, abroad, that he would never come back. It was 1999. The war in Kosova had just ended. And everyone was just leaving because...

DAD For young men like Alfred in these mountains, it is still not safe.

DRITAN Why isn't it safe? I don't understand.

DAD Revenge.

MUM The wounds of the war are not healed yet.

DAD They will never be.

MUM People are still burning houses, destroying crops and slaughtering herds on both sides of the border.

DAD Slitting throats and bellies open.

MUM The peace is not yet peace.

> **MUM** *and* **DAD** *enter.* **ALFRED** *goes with* **DAD.**

DRITAN/CHORUS Alfred is fourteen years old. My dad didn't tell my mum he was leaving because he knew –

DAD She would never have let it happen if I told her.

DRITAN/CHORUS But I saw. In the middle of the night I got up to go to the toilet and I saw him. From the window.

I watch him and my Dad go up the road towards the bus stop.

Until he disappears... And then that night, my mum says.

MUM Ibish, where is Alfred?

DAD I told you. He's down south with my uncle.

...Bute, I sent him away. To England. It will be okay. He's smart. He will do well there.

DRITAN/CHORUS My mum went crazy.

MUM *finds and loads the magazine in the AK-47.*

MUM Why?

DAD He wanted to go.

MUM Why did you say yes? Why didn't you talk about it with me?

DAD Would you have agreed...?

MUM Bring him back.

DAD What is there for him here? Except violence?

MUM You will bring him back now.

DAD You know I can't... He knows what he's doing. He's fourteen / years old.

MUM Exactly. He's a child.

DAD Not for much longer. And then what? You want him to grow into a man, a good man with a long life, don't you? Do you really think he can do that here? What is this country now? What is there for him here now except hunting and being hunted? Somewhere else, maybe he has a chance... If you're going to shoot me you need to point the gun at me.

MUM Don't worry I know how to shoot you. I did military service too. Never forget that...

She lowers the gun.

DRITAN/CHORUS Maybe a week later we had a phone call.

DAD Hello.

DRITAN/CHORUS I'd never ever seen my Dad look hurt before.

DRITAN Dad, What's wrong?

DAD Shut up.

MUM Shhh.

DAD Alfred is stuck in France.

MUM He's run out of money.

DAD Once he got across the sea. Once he got his feet on land, I thought he'd be alright but...

DRITAN But what?

MUM He's stuck near Calais. And we have no way of getting any money to him.

DAD He can't move. I should have given him more money.

DRITAN/CHORUS It took Alfred over two months to get to England. An Albanian friend in England finally sent him the money to get across the English Channel.

Besa: "if you can help someone, help them".

4. Relentless

DRITAN *and his gang.*

DRITAN/CHORUS I had a gang, like Alfred.

Not a street gang. Just a group of friends.

There are rules: you can't walk away from a fight; you get more respect if you lose than if you walk away.

First, it's just playing around with your brother or whatever. He slaps you around until you start defending yourself.

Slowly, you get into it...

You scrap within your own gang. For nothing. Just for fun.

But when you fought with other gangs that was serious – you'd have to really beat the shit out of them for real.

But fighting within your own gang was like, training.

Now, I think, what the fuck?

A boy, **RICKY***, enters.*

The thing with fights in my culture is, there is very little talking.

You just look at each other.

And in that moment, as you look at your opponent, you "Ja han zemren": ja han zemren – "eat his heart".

That's what we call it.

They look into each others' eyes.

Knock the stuffing out of him before you strike a blow.

And he's trying to do the same to you.

They eat each others' hearts.

My first proper fight was with this boy, Ricky. Neither Ricky or me wanted to fight each other. Because we was related. Well, our mums were, somehow. In my culture, family is everything. We say:

MUM Without family, you are nothing.

DRITAN/CHORUS But me and Ricky had to fight.

Because you can't back down, right? I don't know which one of us said yes to this or what started it. But once we started, we couldn't walk away.

RICKY *and* DRITAN *fight. Slap for slap. They get hurt. They don't stop.*

Maybe it was fun.

But then

Suddenly

I don't like this.

It felt like...a week

This fight.

I don't like this.

But

In this family

You never quit.

I don't like this.

When you are hit

Get back up.

Hit harder

Until

Eventually...

The fight is over. But there is no handshake.

DRITAN Fuck you, Ricky.

RICKY No. Fuck you, Dritan.

DRITAN/CHORUS Relentless.

For what?

For nothing.

5. School

DRITAN/CHORUS But the best idea is not to fight. Or at least not yourself. At school I was clever. Especially at maths. I suppose I was kind of the leader, the brains, the one who had all the ideas, the schemes, the bottle to do shit. The only one of us who couldn't add up properly was Andi. But Andi had a special set of skills. He was really strong and he had what we called a "death grip". His thumb had a double turn in it, so that if he grabbed hold of you, his grip locked around your wrist and you couldn't break it no matter what you did. Andi was handy. There was this little dude in my class kept getting up in my face: Genzi. He was little but he was a really hard fighter. I needed to get him before he got me. So I made it into a game.

DRITAN Hey, Genzi, I bet you couldn't take Andi in a fight.

GENZI What you saying? Andi can't fight for shit.

DRITAN Well how about we test that out? Andi says he can knock you out.

GENZI Lunch time. The usual place. Tell him.

DRITAN Hey, Andi, Genzi says he could kill you, man.

ANDI Tell him lunchtime. The usual place.

Lunch time. The usual place. **ANDI** *and* **GENZI** *square up.*

DRITAN Go on. Make a move man.

ANDI I will. I will...

DRITAN Look. Grab his arm with your death grip and punch him in the balls three times.

GENZI Come on, I'm gonna kill you man.

DRITAN Back off. He's warming up, you dick.

GENZI Who you calling a dick? You dick.

ANDI Don't call him a dick, you dick. Don't you fucking dare.

ANDI *seizes* GENZI, *and batters him.* DRITAN *and his mates congratulate,* ANDI.

DRITAN/CHORUS After that Genzi and me were friends. I was never by myself. Everyone plays together. You stick together, even if you don't really like a kid. That's how it is in my country. No kid is ever left out or alone.

6. Dritan Leaves home

DRITAN *and his father.*

DRITAN/CHORUS I don't know why my Dad let me go. Especially now he knew how dangerous it had been for Alfred... I was too young, too weak to make this journey. I wouldn't have sent me. Would you send your kid? ...He wouldn't have sent me unless there was a reason.

DAD Maybe the war is over. But there are still plenty of guns. And plenty of anger and revenge.

DRITAN Who would take revenge on us, Dad? What did we do?

DAD ...

DRITAN/CHORUS He doesn't answer... But months later he finally says...

DAD Tomorrow, you are going to leave school and we're going to travel south to Tirana. We are going to try and get you out of here. To London. To Alfred.

DRITAN Yes!

DAD But don't say anything to anyone. Especially your mother. Because if you tell her...

DRITAN I'll be quiet.

DAD Then be quiet.

DRITAN/CHORUS My mum didn't know.

MUM I did know...

DRITAN/CHORUS If you knew why did you let me go?

MUM He told me. Not when, though.

DRITAN/CHORUS Then why didn't you stop him?

MUM It wasn't in my hands.

DRITAN/CHORUS How wasn't it in your hands?

MUM You don't understand. In our culture, there is an unwritten law which still holds: "when the head of the house makes a decision, ask no questions."

DRITAN/CHORUS	MUM
I don't understand.	
	You don't understand.
She didn't know.	
	I felt bad.
How could she know and do nothing?	
	How was I meant to feel?
She didn't know.	
	Where will he end up?
No.	
	At least he will have Alfred. Alfred had no one At least they will be together.

MUM I knew. But I didn't want to speak it out loud. Because then I would have had to stop you.

DRITAN/CHORUS Didn't you know the danger into which I was going?

MUM I knew the danger you were leaving...

DRITAN/CHORUS What danger?

MUM Everything about this time and place was dangerous for you. Your father didn't tell me how he was sending you. He was very brave to do that. I wouldn't have been so brave. If I'd known how he was sending you through the boats system like your brother, I wouldn't have let you go.

Tirana. Noise of the big city. **DRITAN** *and his father meet the* **BIG BOSS**.

DRITAN/CHORUS Tirana: Capital of Albania.

Me and my Dad meet the main dude of the mafia gang – the Boss. His gang are going to smuggle me to England.

DAD How's it going?

BIG BOSS Good. How are things back home Up North?

DAD Worse than before. Much worse.

BIG BOSS Then you are making the right decision.

DAD *(he hands the* **BOSS** *an envelope)* Here. Like I said, I will get you the rest / of the money when –

BIG BOSS Don't worry, my friend. Okay?

DRITAN He helped us because he was from Up North like us. Up North's the same everywhere isn't it? Not the same as down south.

BIG BOSS I help because I respect your mother. And your father. He has done much for the Albanian cause in Kosova.

DRITAN What's he done?

DAD Shut up. We don't talk about these things.

DRITAN Back then in Albania, mafia wasn't always all about money. This guy was also about helping people. And everyone liked him for it.

BIG BOSS Okay, let's get moving. Dritan, you okay?

DRITAN Don't worry about me, dude. I'm fine.

> **MAFIA DUDE** *enters.*

BIG BOSS *(laughs)* Little shit, eh? This is your driver. You go with him. He's going to drive you and these other guys to where you get the boat.

DAD So you've got everything, right?

DRITAN Yes.

DAD Where's your money?

DRITAN/CHORUS ...This time, my Dad's learned from what happened to my brother and he's given me plenty of money to make sure I can get to England. But what am I going to do with it?

I might lose it. Or someone will steal it... *(To* DAD*)* Here.

DAD Good... When you get to London, go to Alfred. He's in Ilford. He knows you're coming okay? At least you'll have your brother. He's settled, he'll look after you.

DRITAN I'll be alright, Dad.

DAD Of course you will... And Dritan... Remember, learn all you can from the British, but don't become like them. Not with regard to family anyway. Because without / family –

DRITAN Without family you're nothing. I know, Dad.

DAD ...So... I'm going to go now... Goodbye then.

DRITAN Yeah, bye. See ya.

DRITAN/CHORUS I say, "See ya", as if I am just popping down to the river for a swim and I'll be home for dinner.

They hug. His DAD *leaves.*

I had to start quickly, to get used to being alone.

And I'm only a little kid.

Just eleven years old.

In the van.

There's about twelve of us in this van.

I'm the only kid.

But even though I'm only a kid, I can see this is a well-oiled operation.

None of the gang members knows each other so they can never grass on or betray each other. They only know their bit of the plan.

And the Boss's name.

But they're never going to tell anyone that.

So we drive.

And drive. It takes five hours before we reach the port of Vlora.

It's night time...

There's another mafia dude waiting for us.

2ND MAFIA DUDE Are you people with the Boss? Yeah? Hey kid, you the Boss's little bastard?

DRITAN No, man. He's my bastard.

2ND MAFIA DUDE What? What is he saying I can't understand his accent?

DRITAN I said, "He's my bastard."

Everyone laughs.

2ND MAFIA DUDE What's so fucking funny? Are you his kid or not?

OTHER REFUGEES – Cocky little shit.

– Little boy taking the piss out of this mafia dude.

– Careful, kid, you want to be careful.

DRITAN/CHORUS And then...we get to this hotel.

OTHER REFUGEES – Hey kid. Wrap your stuff.

– Get plastic bags and wrap your clothes and shit.

– So it doesn't get wet if you have to swim for it.

DRITAN *takes his clothes from a small sports bag and wraps them. He wraps his wallet and puts it inside his track suit bottoms and tucks those into his socks and pulls jeans on over these.*

DRITAN/CHORUS It's about four in the morning.

Black dark.

Now we're at the dock.

And there is our boat.

Forty-five of us get packed into that boat.

But I can tell it's meant for much less people.

And these boats man...

They're not safe.

Nothing to hold onto.

No life jackets.

MAFIA DUDE Get in, kid.

DRITAN *(to the* **MAFIA DUDE***)* The boat's already full.

MAFIA DUDES – Just hurry up and sit down, little shit.

　– Wait, You're the Boss's kid, right?

DRITAN Yeah.

1ST MAFIA DUDE Sit here. By the driver. It's the safest place. Less turbulence. *(To a female passenger)* You. Move. Let the kid sit here.

They move a woman to give him a seat.

DRITAN But what about that lady? I can't take her seat.

2ND MAFIA DUDE Mind your own fucking business and just fucking move. We're looking after you. You're not looking after anyone, understand? Sit down.

　DRITAN *sits.*

DRITAN/CHORUS The boat starts and we pull away.

But there's this...

Smell...

Of...

Petrol...

I hate...

The smell of...

　DRITAN *vomits all over the boat.*

I couldn't throw up over the side.

Cos I just knew that if I fell off, they wasn't coming back
for me.

The boat bounces through the waves. Then, **POLICE**
sirens. Suddenly, the engine stops. **DRITAN** *jumps into
the water.*

It's cold.

The sea.

And it's too deep for a little kid

Forward Forward Forward

Or nothing

Or down

He swims.

Go go go

I didn't know if

Til my feet touched the floor

The **PASSENGERS** *run from the* **POLICE***. They are chased.
They are caught. Including* **DRITAN***.*

I'm in a police station. Me and some others – I am the only
kid – are put in a cell. Like a massive cell. No beds. And I'm
soaking wet. I'm just a little kid and they didn't give me any
dry clothes or nothing. And it's late, and I'm...

He falls asleep. Later, a **POLICEMAN** *wakes him up.
He hands* **DRITAN** *a mobile phone.*

POLICE Pssssst. Take this.

DRITAN What the fuck's going on?

POLICE Just take the fucking phone. Now.

The phone rings.

DRITAN Hello...

BIG BOSS Dritan, it's me. I'm outside the police station. They're going to open the door for you and you're going to walk straight out.

DRITAN I can't walk out of jail / I –

BIG BOSS The policeman who gave you the phone is going to give you some money to buy some bread.

Take the money, walk out the door. I'll pick you up.

The **POLICEMAN** *takes back his phone and hands* **DRITAN** *some money.*

POLICE For bread. Piss off.

DRITAN *takes the money. The cell door opens and he walks past the* **POLICEMAN**. *Outside the* **POLICE** *station, the* **BOSS** *waits.*

DRITAN What about everyone else?

BIG BOSS What about them? They'll be fine. Let's go. Let's get something to eat.

DRITAN Are we going to eat here? Right in front of the police station?

BIG BOSS We'll take you back to the hotel and we'll try again tonight. Here, kid. Take this. My number is programmed into it. If you have a problem, / an emergency –

DRITAN/CHORUS Wow a mobile phone. I have always wanted a mobile phone. I've always wanted a Nokia.

DRITAN Thank you...

DRITAN *wraps up the mobile phone in plastic bags and hides it in his trousers.*

DRITAN/CHORUS Four a.m.

Another boat.

Everything's different

Every single mafia dude is carrying a gun.

The boat's packed.

It's a rush.

I'm at the front.

And at the front

It's totally different to

The back

The waves hit the front of the boat. **DRITAN** *is thrown up in the air and slammed to the floor. This happens multiple times. It's painful.*

I am eleven years old and I am going to die.

DRITAN *grabs hold of a guy beside him who wears a leather jacket. Every time he is thrown in the air, he almost chokes the guy with the collar of the jacket. The guy tries to shake him off.* **DRITAN** *clings on.*

LEATHER JACKET GUY Get off me.

DRITAN No.

LEATHER JACKET GUY Get off.

DRITAN/CHORUS No way, man...

I held onto that dude for six hours.

The boat bounces. The slamming continues.

7. The Donkey

Back home: a memory. **DRITAN** *is on a tractor.*

DRITAN/CHORUS During the war when refugees started fleeing, my dad bought a tractor off one of the people passing through our village. It was a wreck – no seats, no mudguards, just a place to stand. I dunno why he bought it. We didn't need a tractor. We called it "The Donkey", cos you'd bounce around on it all over the place. My brother wouldn't touch it. He was too scared. But my dad let me drive it. I was nine years old.

DAD *sits on the tractor.*

DAD Okay, Dritan, come on then. Come up here. *(DRITAN climbs up)* Calm down, now. Concentrate. Now... You steer okay.

DRITAN Yeah, no problem.

DAD I'll work the gears. Ready.

DRITAN Go. Yes. I said, "Go", Dad.

DAD *starts the tractor. They bounce around.*

Whoah...

DAD It's okay. You're doing great.

DRITAN What if I crash?

DAD You won't crash. I'm with you.

DRITAN I can't do it.

DAD Dritan... Listen: I trust you. Okay?

DRITAN Okay.

DRITAN *drives.*

DAD See. You can do this.

DRITAN/CHORUS I can do this.

DAD You are doing this...

They laugh.

8. Second Leg of Journey: Italy I

The boat. Bouncing.

DRITAN/CHORUS ...I'm doing this, Dad.

I am doing it.

Over there: land.

Italy.

But we go up and down the coast for ages.

Ages.

Cos the police are trying to catch us...

The **POLICE** *boat chases the mafia boat. The* **MAFIA DUDES** *all drew their guns.*

So, this is why all the mafia dudes have guns.

I didn't know this then, but I know now these boats weren't just carrying people, they were carrying drugs too. Us refugees weren't just extra cash. We were a human shield. And that's why the police didn't shoot at the boat.

MAFIA DUDE Jump.

DRITAN *jumps, holding his bag.*

DRITAN/CHORUS Whoah.

Panic panic panic panic

The other people jump from the boat. He swims. Around him, people screaming, crying, trying to stay afloat. Some people can't swim.

People screaming all around me.

Why would you get in a boat if you can't swim?

I'm going to look after me.

Go go go

Or nothing

Or down

He swims.

Forward Forward Forward

Til my feet touched the

Beach.

Rocky beach.

Ow.

Why did my Dad do this to me?

The Italian gang members meet them on the beach.
DRITAN *is wet and shivering.*

MAFIA DUDE You the Boss's people, yeah? Follow us. Come on. Hurry hurry hurry. Take off your wet clothes. Leave them here.

DRITAN An abandoned building.

Loads of clothes everywhere...

MAFIA DUDE Put on dry clothes. If the police see you soaking wet they'll know you're illegal. Hurry.

DRITAN *changes his clothes, unwrapping them from the plastic bags within his football bag.*

DRITAN Who are you?

MAFIA DUDE Doesn't matter. I'm "blind".

DRITAN What do you mean, you're blind? / How can you take us anywhere?

MAFIA DUDE It means I don't fucking see you, you don't fucking see me. Just shut the fuck up and move. Quickly.

DRITAN/CHORUS They take us into the forest.

MAFIA DUDE Okay, this is where you sleep. No one will see you here.

DRITAN/CHORUS It's winter. It's freezing cold. I have warm clothes but it's...not...enough...

And then I remember, my dad always said:

DAD Don't sleep on your back, because the cold will get into your lungs quicker. If you sleep somewhere rough always sleep on your front with your arms underneath you.

DRITAN *adjusts his sleeping position. He shivers. A man,* **JIMMY,** *lies next to him.*

DRITAN/CHORUS And I can see this dude lying opposite. He's older. And he's just staring at me. Looking...

What's he looking at...? Where's my wallet...?

Okay. Sleep... But it's too cold to sleep but I'm...so... Tired...

MAFIA DUDE Wake up! Boy. Taxi's here. Move.

DRITAN *gets up.*

You go with these guys in the next car, okay?

DRITAN Okay.

JIMMY Wait. This kid is with me. I'm with him. I am going in this car.

MAFIA DUDE Shut up. We will tell you/what car...

JIMMY I'm telling you, I'm looking after this kid. And he's not leaving without me.

DRITAN/CHORUS This is the starey dude. What does he want?

MAFIA DUDE What the... Look, I don't give a shit... Is he with you kid...? Is he with you?

DRITAN *and* **JIMMY** *look at each other.*

9. Reading People

A memory. **DRITAN** *and* **DAD.**

DRITAN/CHORUS From a little kid, my Dad would say to me:

DAD Don't take shit from anyone.

DRITAN/CHORUS In my country you get taught how to read people, physically. It's all about energy.

DAD Just watch people very closely... Watch a guy, how he speaks. How he looks at you. What does it mean? See if you can see the same thing in anyone else.

DRITAN *and the* **CHORUS** *study each other's energy.*

DRITAN/CHORUS And I'd make like a mental list. I dunno, like when someone says:

"I really like you."

Watch how their head turns aside. That means they're taking the piss. I don't know how to explain it. Most people pick this skill up gradually, socially. My Dad trained me for it.

DAD Watch for the energy people give. See the real intention behind someone's action.

DRITAN/CHORUS To me it was like a mission. I'd make lists of what different looks and gestures meant, mostly in my head...

DAD Especially if you live in a place like this where there's a lot of manipulating. And a lot of danger. You need to know if you can trust a person, Dritan.

DRITAN/CHORUS But if anything was complicated, I'd write it down because otherwise I'd forget.

DAD Remember: this is for defence.

10. Italy: Part II

DRITAN *reads* JIMMY.

JIMMY I'm telling you, I'm looking after this kid. And he's not leaving without me.

MAFIA DUDE Is he with you kid?

DRITAN ...Yeah. He's with me.

MAFIA DUDE Okay. *(To* DRITAN*)* You – sit back down again. You'll go in the next car.

DRITAN *(to* JIMMY*)* Ah... What'd you do that for? We've missed our chance.

JIMMY There'll be more taxis. Just you wait. We've paid our money, remember.

They wait.

DRITAN What's your name?

JIMMY Gzim... But you can call me Jimmy. That's what everybody in England calls me. That's where you're going, yes?

DRITAN Yeah.

DRITAN/CHORUS He speaks English. This could be handy. I'm thinking – I know he's going to use me.

But maybe I can use him too.

Gang member returns.

MAFIA DUDE Get in this car and go to Bari train station. Get the train to Milan. Someone will meet you there. Go.

DRITAN Bari? Where is Bari? *(They are in Bari train station)* Bari. Train station. And it's...huge. And there's just thousands of people and hundreds of trains and... This random Albanian guy with curly hair walks up to me and Jimmy and says...

MAFIA DUDE You the Boss's people?

JIMMY Yeah.

MAFIA DUDE I'm going to get your tickets to Milan. So that's gonna be one hundred and ninety euros.

JIMMY But we paid for these in advance.

DRITAN Yeah. My dad paid for all the tickets. All-inclusive price, he said.

MAFIA DUDE If you don't want to give me your money, then you stay here.

DRITAN Alright.

> **DRITAN** *takes out his wallet and counts out the money. The guy takes it.*

MAFIA DUDE And give me any of your money from home. I'll exchange it for you. You're not going to need it. I'll get you euros. How much have you got?

DRITAN This much.

MAFIA DUDE I'll give you twenty euros for that.

DRITAN Bullshit. This is worth way more than twenty euros. That's not fair. Maths is my thing, man.

This much is worth a hundred euros. You think I'm stupid. Fucking thief.

MAFIA DUDE You can't spend your country's money here, you need euros.

DRITAN I told you, my dad paid all-inclusive for the train tickets, now you're charging me for the train tickets and now you want my other money too. Fuck off.

MAFIA DUDE Little bastard, get to Milan by yourself.

> *The* **MAFIA DUDE** *starts walking away.* **DRITAN** *takes out his phone. He dials a number.*

DRITAN Right. This isn't good enough. This isn't what I paid for. Bad service, dude. I'm phoning the Boss.

MAFIA DUDE What you doing, little shit...? *(To* JIMMY*)* He's taking the piss right.

The call connects. The BOSS *answers.*

BIG BOSS Hello. Who is this?

DRITAN It's me. It's Dritan.

BIG BOSS What's the problem, little man?

DRITAN I'm sick of this. My dad paid you for this trip and it's shit. I'm freezing and my taxi was late.

BIG BOSS That's not a problem. You call me when there's an actual/ problem.

DRITAN And now this bastard's trying to rip me off. He's taken a hundred and ninety euros off me and now he wants all my other money. We paid up front. My dad paid for everything. Why are all your people trying to rip us off? This is a formal complaint.

BIG BOSS Calm down, kid... I understand. Is this guy still with you? Put him on the phone.

DRITAN *hands the phone to the curly-headed dude.*

DRITAN/CHORUS The Boss wants to talk to you.

MAFIA DUDE *(on the phone)* Yes... Yes... No... Yes. *(Handing the phone back to* DRITAN*)* He wants to talk to you.

DRITAN *takes the phone.*

BIG BOSS Listen, little man, it's sorted. Get to Milan. I'll make sure the best guy I know meets you there. Okay?

DRITAN Okay. Thank you. Bye.

DRITAN *hangs up.*

MAFIA DUDE Why the hell did you do that you little shit? Do you know what you've done?

DRITAN Just get me my tickets. Please. Immediately.

DRITAN/CHORUS And he does. Right away.

And now we're on the train to Milan.

TICKET INSPECTOR Tickets, please. All tickets please...

DRITAN *falls asleep.*

Milano. Milano. All change please. All change at Milano.

They leave the train.

DRITAN/CHORUS It's eleven o'clock at night. I can't see anyone...

MAFIA DUDE You're the Boss' kid right?

DRITAN/CHORUS Yeah. This dude's rich. He's very well dressed. Nice hair. Like a millionaire.

MAFIA DUDE The Boss said I have to take special care of you, as you've not had good customer service. Who's this?

DRITAN Jimmy. He's with me.

MAFIA DUDE I don't need to know his name. But okay, come with me. Get in the car, please, sirs...

DRITAN/CHORUS Now we're getting the red-carpet, luxury treatment. It always pays to complain... And this new mafia dude is suave. Posh. Speaks proper Albanian. And he's straight up.

MAFIA DUDE Look, boys, trust no one. Not even me. Everyone will try to rip you off. And I will as well. No hard feelings. Don't look back. Just forward. All you need to do is keep going forward to your destination. Just keep moving.

DRITAN/CHORUS He drives us all night. Through the border. Into Switzerland. It's nice and warm in this car. And outside, it's snowing. And I relax for the first time since I slept in my own bed. And I...

He falls asleep.

11. Paris to Belgium to Strood

DRITAN *wakes up.*

DRITAN/CHORUS I wake up and
Paris.

The rich dude's pulled up outside of some big train station.

MAFIA DUDE Okay, boys. You go in there and you buy a ticket to Brussels. The price should be about eighty euros. Get to Brussels and someone will meet you there. They will take you to a lorry and that lorry will get you to London. Okay?

DRITAN Okay.

MAFIA DUDE And now you will each give me one hundred euros. Expenses, yeah? (**DRITAN** *hands over the money)* No hard feelings. Just keep going forwards. Goodbye.

The car drives off.

DRITAN/CHORUS And I'm looking in my wallet and it's starting to look empty. They shouldn't be asking us for this. We already paid. Anyway, he did say he'd rip us off... Jimmy and me go to the ticket office.

TICKET SELLER Comment puis-je t'aider?

DRITAN I want to go to Brussels.

TICKET SELLER Je ne comprends pas. Où veux tu aller?

DRITAN What? I don't understand. Brussels. I want to go to Brussels?

TICKET SELLER Ah, vous voulez aller à Bruxelles? Billet simple ou aller-retour ?

DRITAN What? I just want a train ticket. Look. One hundred euros.

TICKET SELLER Mais c'est trop d'argent. Un billet de retour coûte quatre-vingts euros.

DRITAN Just take the money. Fuck's sake...

The cashier hands over the tickets. They try to hand over change but **DRITAN** *runs for the train.*

TICKET SELLER Attendez! Votre monnaie!

DRITAN/CHORUS I still don't know what any of that was about... So, we get on the train to Brussels and this is the shortest part of the trip. Whoosh – we're there. And some new mafia dude picks us up and drives us. To a restaurant.

JIMMY It's not a restaurant, Dritan.

DRITAN/CHORUS To a pub then.

JIMMY It's not a pub.

We, my young friend, are in a strip club.

The strip club. Music. Lights. Alcohol... Exotic Dancers.

12. Sisters

DRITAN/CHORUS Both of my sisters are older than me and my brother. My younger big sister is called Tila. Tila is quiet, laid-back, kind. Like Alfred. And she has beautiful handwriting. It's so beautiful that people come and ask her to write letters for them. And she listens to you when you talk about your day, and how you feel and stuff. But my oldest sister... She is called Luli. Her name means "flower" but she is tough, man, tough. She's eleven years older than me. When I was little, she was the household woman, she would run everything while my mum was at work – cook, clean, I even seen her fix broken shit and that – lightbulbs, plugs, fuses, everything. And she could fight as well. All the boys at school were scared of Luli. Yeah, she scared me too. One time when I was very little, we was all watching TV together... Everyone had a satellite dish. If you turned it this way, you got TV from Eastern Europe, but if you turned it this way...

LULI, TILA, ALFRED *and* **DRITAN** *watch TV.*

DRITAN I don't understand a word of this.

LULI Of course you don't. It's in Italian.

DRITAN Why are we watching Italian TV? I wanna watch cartoons.

TILA Shhh... Michele's so handsome.

LULI Tell me about it.

DRITAN Him? He looks like a donkey.

LULI Tan, you say another word and I'll...

DRITAN You'll what?

ALFRED Dritan, shut up. She's going to get mad.

DRITAN Do you wanna watch this shit?

ALFRED No.

DRITAN Then, say something. It's our TV too...

ALFRED I'm staying out of it.

DRITAN Who's he then? The old man that ugly Michele you like is talking to?

TILA He's a mafia dude. Proper gangster. Tano Carridi. / But Michele... So gorgeous.

LULI So gorgeous.

DRITAN Tano. Like me. Tan. He's really cool. Does he hate that ugly guy? He looks like he wants to kill him. I can tell: it's his energy.

LULI I'm going to slap your head off in a minute.

TILA Yes because he wants control of the bank.

LULI Will you all – everyone – just shut up. I'm trying to watch this. *(To* DRITAN*)* You. Not. Another. Word.

DRITAN ...Piss. Right. Off.

LULI What did you say to me?

TILA Leave him alone, Luli. He's only little.

DRITAN I said: Piss. Right. Off.

LULI *goes for* DRITAN.

TILA No, I'm not going to let you. *(*TILA *restrains* LULI. *To* DRITAN *and* ALFRED*)* Boys, hold her legs.

They pile on top of LULI. *She wrestles them.*

ALFRED Luli, this isn't my idea. I don't want to do this.

LULI Get off me. I am going to kill you all.

DRITAN/CHORUS I'm getting more and more scared because she's really angry and if we let her go...the world is going to end. I almost want to cry I am so frightened. But Tila is just laughing. And laughing.

13. Brussels to England

The strip club - women laughing. Lights, music, exotic dancers. JIMMY *buys a beer, watches the girls. Another little boy sits at the bar.*

DRITAN/CHORUS Jimmy likes the strip club. Sort of. I think it's pretty boring, actually. And I ain't never seen a woman dressed...or not dressed...like that before. What are they doing?

RICKY They're exotic dancing. It's their job. And it's an art form.

DRITAN/CHORUS Another little kid a bit younger than me puts his arm around my shoulders.

RICKY My mum says women who do that are either drug addicts or whores but Sabine says that's just because my mum don't know shit.

DRITAN/CHORUS Ricky? Is this little Ricky from back home?

RICKY Cos Sabine says a stripper is a beautiful, intelligent, educated, sexually empowered woman who treats her job as a job and not a party.

DRITAN/CHORUS Bloody hell, it is Ricky. What the hell is he doing here?

RICKY Hi, Dritan. Would you like a drink? It's my round.

DRITAN/CHORUS Things haven't really been the same between Ricky and me since we had that relentless fight when he was eight and I was nine. But now, I'm glad to see him. Cos he's family. Somehow.

DRITAN What the hell are you doing here?

RICKY Same as you: waiting for them to come and get me. I've been waiting here three days.

DRITAN Three days? Where do you sleep? Eat?

RICKY Yeah. I sleep on the sofas over there. And Sabine brings me croissants for breakfast and hot dogs for dinner every day. And I buy her Singapore Slings. It's an agreement.

DRITAN Who's Sabine?

> **RICKY** *points to one of the exotic dancers.*

Are you stupid or what...? You can't stay here with her. I'm not waiting here three days. I'm going to England.

RICKY So am I. Whenever they come get me. Just no one's come got me yet.

DRITAN There's a password, Rick. The mafia dude who comes for you will say the password.

RICKY Oh. Don't remember it.

DRITAN How much money you got left?

RICKY Fifty euros.

DRITAN Fifty? That's not much, man.

RICKY Yeah but cocktails are bloody expensive, mate.

DRITAN/CHORUS I can see Ricky needs my help. And I'm older – he is ten and I am eleven. So, it's up to me to look after him.

DRITAN When they come for us, we can take you with us... Unless you want to stay here.

RICKY Not really. Sabine's really nice and everything. But it's pretty boring here. And it's dark all the time. And this music is really shit.

DRITAN/CHORUS The music is really shit. We wait in the strip club about an hour. I swear, it was the longest hour of my life. So boring... And then:

> **MAFIA DUDE** *enters.*

This is our guy.

He says the password.

And we're in a lorry with big massive rolls of carpets and lots of refugees, and lots of them are Kurdish people. There's nowhere to hide...

The driver shuts the door.

It's pitch black.

So, we lie on the carpets and hold on.

The lorry starts. They all tumble about in the lorry. The **KURDISH PEOPLE** *scream.*

OTHER REFUGEES	KURDS
– Shut the fuck up.	– Bavê me yê li ezmanan, Bila navê te pîroz be. Bila padîşahiya te bê. –
– Why are you screaming?	Daxwaza te wek li ezmanan, Li ser rûyê erdê jî bi cih bê. Nanê me yê rojane roj bi roj bide me.
– You're gonna get us caught.	Û li deynên me bibihûre,
	Wek ku em li deyndarên xwe bihûrtine. Û me nebe ceribandinê, Lê me ji yê xerab xilas bike. Amîn.
– Shut up or I will smash your fucking head in.	

The lorry rocks as the ferry rocks in the waves. People roll about. More screaming, crying, praying.

DRITAN/CHORUS I don't know how long we are in the lorry. It feels like days. You can't talk, you can't eat, you can't go to the toilet. And it's so dark... It feels like...forever. And then...

Silence. Sound of seagulls.

England.

The **KURDISH PEOPLE** *start banging on the cab of the lorry. The lorry stops.* **POLICE** *sirens. The door opens, light and sound pour in.*

POLICE Police! Everybody out. Now.

Everyone runs.

JIMMY Don't run, boys. Sssh. Just be calm. Walk. Let's cross the street and keep walking. Like we belong here.

DRITAN/CHORUS And so we walk. And walk. Where the hell are we?

S-T-R-O-O-D ... Strood.

Where the hell is that? What are we going to do?

Get the train to London.

How far is it? How much does that cost?

They should have taken us all the way, man.

JIMMY Yeah, well, this is where we are, boys. How much you got? I gave all mine away in Paris to that posh dude. Tell you what, you boys give your money, I'll buy tickets for all of us to get to London.

DRITAN/CHORUS And I look at Jimmy. Trying to read his energy. Will he come back? Will he leave us here?

DRITAN Give him your money, Ricky... Give it to him... We need him.

RICKY *hands over his money.* **DRITAN** *hands over this money. And* **JIMMY** *walks away. They wait.*

JIMMY Right, lads. Platform four in five minutes. Move it.

DRITAN/CHORUS I knew Jimmy would come back.

An hour later and we're in King's Cross. And Jimmy's...gone.

Just me and Ricky now. Alone. And there's so many people and so much...language and letters and names of places I don't understand. And I'm starving and Ricky's –

RICKY Starving.

DRITAN/CHORUS What do I do now? I am eleven years old, and Ricky is ten and we are stuck...

ALBANIAN GUY Hey, you guys. You just arrived yeah?

DRITAN/CHORUS Some random Albanian-speaking guy stops beside us.

ALBANIAN GUY Ah, you're from Up North, yeah? You got family here? Do you know where they live?

DRITAN Ilford.

ALBANIAN GUY There's a pub called The Brown Bear on Ryecroft Road. Tell them your brother's name and they will find him. Here's some money. This'll be enough for two train tickets. And some crisps.

DRITAN Thank you. What's your name. I'll find you. Pay you back.

ALBANIAN GUY Doesn't matter. If you can help someone, then why not?

DRITAN/CHORUS Besa... And he's gone. And now we have to get train tickets. With no English. So I just say "Ilford" and point at me and Ricky... And half an hour later...

The Brown Bear pub. Music. Beer. Men.

MEN IN BAR – Hey, little man, what are you doing in here?

   – What's his name?

   – Kastrati.

   – There are lots of Kastratis.

   – Alfred Kastrati. Anyone here know Alfred Kastrati?

   – You got his number...? Ring him. Tell him his little brother's here.

Someone calls **ALFRED.**

DRITAN/CHORUS The whole journey has only taken four days from Vlora to Ilford. But it feels like four weeks...

ALFRED *arrives. They look at each other.*

Is that my brother? He looks different. He's got a moustache. He's bigger – like, a man now. Seventeen... Of course it's my –

ALFRED Look at you, all grown up... Dad told me you were coming. I just didn't know when... Are you okay?

DRITAN/CHORUS Am I okay? I don't know... I am okay. Now that Alfred is here. Now that I am with Alfred, I will be okay.

ALFRED Well, come here, you little shit.

They hug.

14. Ilford and Alfred

DRITAN/CHORUS The next morning, Alfred walks me through Ilford.

DRITAN Is this London?

ALFRED Yeah. Not the centre, but, yeah, you're in London, little man.

DRITAN/CHORUS This isn't the London I expected. This is small little rows of cramped houses they called "terraced". They look like chicken huts. And everything's dirty. But I am with Alfred.

ALFRED Come on. You've got to get registered.

DRITAN/CHORUS I'm in this big office building, in a room that looks like one of those cells off a cop show where the detectives interrogate people. And –

CHORUS Alfred's not allowed in there with him.

DRITAN I am just a little kid. I don't know what's happening but –

SOLICITOR I'm your solicitor.

INTERPRETER This is your solicitor. I'm your interpreter. And this is –

IMMIGRATION OFFICER I represent Her Majesty's Home Office.

CHORUS Dritan doesn't know what is happening. He doesn't know why he is here.

IMMIGRATION OFFICER/INTERPETER *(not exactly at the same time)* Where are you from?

Where were you born?

How old are you?

Who are your parents?

How did you travel here?

CHORUS Dritan is scared. He doesn't know if he has been arrested. Where is his brother?

DRITAN Have they arrested me? Why have they arrested me?

SOLICITOR/INTERPRETER *(not exactly at the same time)* They haven't arrested you. Just answer their questions. Just give direct answers to what they ask. Don't say anything more than they ask you, okay?

IMMIGRATION OFFICER/INTERPETER *(not exactly at the same time)* Who brought you here?

Why did you come here?

Who were these people?

Were there any other immigrants travelling with you?

CHORUS Dritan wants to cry. He's only little and it seems like this immigration officer is very, very angry with him.

IMMIGRATION OFFICER/ INTERPETER *(not exactly at the same time)*	CHORUS
How big was the boat?	
	Dritan doesn't know the answers.
	But the officer doesn't stop.
Who brought you here?	
	He just wants to cry.
Why did you come here?	
	His eyes start to sting.
Can you remember what they looked like?	
	But he's not going to cry.
Are you lying to us?	
	Forward forward forward
Can you remember?	
	Or nothing

I think you might be lying
to us.

>   Or down.

Who?
Why would you lie?

>   He isn't lying.

>   But there is a system.

Where?

>   And the system has
>   procedures.

Who?

>   Procedures must be
>   followed.

Who?

>   Procedures keep everyone
>   safe.

Who?

The interview picture breaks. **DRITAN** *and* **ALFRED**.

ALFRED Are you alright?

DRITAN I want to go home.

ALFRED You are home, mate. You're with me.

DRITAN/CHORUS I am home. I'm with my brother.

ALFRED's *house. Party time.*

Alfred and me hang out at a house with four other boys
from my country.

And they all work and work and work, every day, washing
cars. They'd worked so hard and saved so much money that
they'd bought the car wash.

My brother is a business owner, so he has loads of money
and at this house there's people and music and dancing and
fun all the time. And Ricky is there with his cousin. And
Alfred really looks after me.

They play. They eat. They laugh.

POLICE – Okay, Police, everyone, show us some ID please.

– And who are you? Why haven't you got any ID?

DRITAN/CHORUS I don't know what they are saying to me, but I think's it's something to do with ID. And now they are asking Alfred lots of questions.

ALFRED Alfred Kastrati... Seventeen... He's my little brother... He's eleven... I am. I am looking after him.

POLICE Right, well, you are both going to need to come down the station with us.

ALFRED What? Why? We haven't done anything.

DRITAN Alfred, what are they saying?

ALFRED Don't worry, little man, it'll be alright. I'll look after you. Come on, we have to go with them.

15. Taken Away

At the POLICE *station.*

CHORUS Dritan doesn't understand what is happening. The police take him to the station.

INTERPRETER This is your social worker. I am your interpreter.

SOCIAL WORKER Blah blah blah blah blah blah blah.

INTERPRETER She says you can't stay with your brother anymore.

SOCIAL WORKER Blah blah. Blah blah blah blah blah blah. Blah. Blah. Blah.

INTERPRETER She is saying Alfred is too young to look after you.

DRITAN My dad told him to look after me. She can kiss my ass. You can kiss my ass, lady.

INTERPRETER *(to* SOCIAL WORKER*)* Blah? Blah blah blah. Blah. Blah blah blah blah blah blah. Blah. Blah. Blah. Blah.

CHORUS Dritan can tell the translator isn't translating what he's actually saying.

And he can tell the social worker doesn't care what he is saying anyway.

He is reading their energy.

INTERPRETER So you're going to go with her/ tonight to stay –

DRITAN Fuck off. I ain't going nowhere except with Alfred.

The SOCIAL WORKER *splits apart* ALFRED *and* DRITAN.

CHORUS The social worker says that she is going to take Dritan to a safe place.

DRITAN Safe place? Alfred is my safe place.

CHORUS No one is listening to Dritan.

There is a system.

And the system has procedures.

Procedures must be followed.

Procedures keep children safe.

The system thinks Alfred is not safe.

The system thinks it has seen Alfred's type before.

The system thinks it doesn't need to investigate its suspicions.

Because Dritan must be kept safe.

Safe is what the system calls "foster care".

In the middle of the night the social worker drives Dritan and Ricky through London.

Dritan is thinking:

"Where are we going?

Are these people going to feed me?

Are these people going to beat me?

Are these people going to rape me?"

What would you think if you were only eleven years old and thrown into a strange house with strange people?

But he cannot tell anyone what he is thinking because he does not have any English words.

He feels

Deaf

And dumb

And blind.

16. Language

Back home: a memory.

DAD Dritan. I bought you some books. Come and look. They're so you can learn English.

DRITAN Why should I learn English?

DAD Sit there and study, Dritan. English is a useful language. You should learn.

CHORUS Now eleven-year-old Dritan wishes he had learned that final lesson his dad was trying to teach nine-year-old him. But then he didn't know he was ever going to England.

DAD You will sit there and do what you are told and learn it.

DRITAN But why do I need to learn it?

DAD You are not going to move, you are not going to look at anything else, you are not going to eat until you have learned that. Even if it takes hours.

CHORUS Dritan remembers doing exactly what his Dad said.

He didn't move. He didn't eat. He just sat there. For hours. And hours.

And he didn't learn a word of English.

Relentless.

17. Foster Care # 1

CHORUS Some social workers put Dritan and Ricky in a car.

RICKY What's happening?

DRITAN Foster care.

RICKY What the hell is foster care?

CHORUS Whatever foster care is, Dritan doesn't think that this is a good way to treat kids. Already he sees that when you are a foster kid, you're treated like a different species to normal kids just cos shit has happened to you. The foster family are Indian: mum, dad and a boy a bit older than me and Ricky. It's the middle of the night and these people have taken them in as an emergency.

FOSTER MUM We're trying to make Dritan and Ricky feel welcome. We're not ready for them because we didn't get any notice. But we'll do our best. They look scared like kids always do when they first come in. We'll try to make them feel safe.

CHORUS But Dritan doesn't feel safe. The foster mother is asking him if he is hungry. But he doesn't understand. She gives them curry to eat. But Dritan has never had curry before and it's too spicy, and so he doesn't eat that. But he can see this foster mum is trying really hard She's showing him his bed... Dritan doesn't feel like he can sleep but he is so tired. The bed is on the floor.

FOSTER MUM I'm so embarrassed that these children have to sleep on the floor. But they couldn't find anyone else to take two little asylum seekers in the middle of the night.

CHORUS Dritan knows it's not her fault. He uses Ricky's mobile to call Alfred.

ALFRED Are you okay?

DRITAN What the fuck is happening?

ALFRED Tan, just calm down, okay. It's going to be alright. Just do everything that they say. I'll find you. I'll come and see you.

DRITAN I want you to come now.

ALFRED I can't come now. If I come now they'll arrest me.

DRITAN But you're my brother. How can they arrest you for just seeing me?

ALFRED Dritan. Listen. You need to calm down. You need to play their game for a while.

DRITAN I don't understand any of this.

ALFRED I know... I know.

DRITAN I'm... What if something...what if people do bad things to me?

ALFRED ...I'll find you. I promise. Now, strong, yeah?

DRITAN Yeah. Of course.

CHORUS Forward forward forward

Or nothing

Or down.

At least he has Ricky...

Until the fourth day.

SOCIAL WORKER Blah blah blah blah blah. Blah blah blah blah blah seaside.

CHORUS The Social worker says they are not staying here. They are moving to another strange house somewhere called "the seaside"

SOCIAL WORKER Blah blah blah blah blah Ricky blah blah blah

SOCIAL WORKERS *pull* **RICKY** *and* **DRITAN** *apart.*

CHORUS Or rather Dritan is going to the seaside. Ricky is staying here.

DRITAN I'm not leaving him.

SOCIAL WORKER Blah blah blah blah blah blah blah.

RICKY No. You can't do this. Dritan...

CHORUS Ricky is crying. Dritan wants to cry. But he can't. He has to be strong now for both of them.

> **DRITAN** *grabs hold of* **RICKY**. *An image of* **RICKY**, *as* **DRITAN** *is pulled away from him.*

Right now Dritan doesn't know this, but he won't see Ricky again. Not for years.

In the car, on the way to the seaside he is thinking:

"Why did my Dad send me here to this country?"

Forward forward forward

Or nothing

Or down.

The seaside

That is an hour away from Alfred. Dritan has timed the drive.

And he wonders why they need to move him so very far away from his brother.

> **SANDRA** *and* **BILL** *enter.*

SANDRA Sandra.

BILL And Bill.

SANDRA And these are our two boys, Stephen and our foster son, Enver.

ENVER Qa bane.

CHORUS At first, Dritan thinks, "Good, another Albanian-speaking boy, we will look after each other." But Enver is not his friend. On the first night, Sandra makes a roast dinner. Dritan hasn't eaten for four days, and he can smell it cooking, all that lovely meat and potatoes and gravy. He is ready for this.

DRITAN *lifts a sausage to his mouth.* **ENVER** *swipes the sausage. He throws it in the bin.*

DRITAN/CHORUS What are you doing? That's my sausage.

ENVER It's pork. We can't eat pork, we're Muslims.

DRITAN Never touch my food again, man. Or I will end your fucking life.

CHORUS Dritan doesn't care if it's pork, he just wants his fucking dinner. Dritan is Muslim, but not religious like this boy. Enver is a traitor too. Stephen, the foster carers' real son, is a bully. Dritan is four, five years younger than him but –

STEPHEN *hurts* **DRITAN.**

DRITAN *(to* **ENVER***)* Tell him to back off. Tell him I'm warning him.

ENVER Hey, Stephen, tell him this. *(Whispers)*

STEPHEN Hey, Dritan. Go fuck your mother.

CHORUS Dritan doesn't know English, but he knows what this means. In his country, you do not talk disrespectfully about people's mothers, or this happens...

DRITAN *beats* **STEPHEN** *up.* **SOCIAL WORKER***s come in and remove* **DRITAN.**

The **SOCIAL WORKERS** *move him really, really far away.*

18. Foster Carers # 2 & #3

CHORUS Where Dritan ends up is the areshole-of-nowhere. With Geoffrey and Anne. And they are...dusty. Everything in this house is covered in dust. And it's too quiet – except for the sound of sheep and tractors. And Geoffrey and Anne do absolutely nothing except watch TV all the time and occasionally ask:

GEOFFREY Alright, Dritan?

ANNE You hungry?

CHORUS

Dritan reads them. Geoffrey and Anne are nice.	**GEOFFREY/ANNE**
	We really are nice. We are. We really do care, don't we?
But they have no interest in him really.	
	You can't allow yourself to get too attached to them. Or them to you.
No interest in themselves.	
	In case they get moved on. You have to keep everything nice and calm. Nice and normal. A routine.
Dritan does not want this routine.	
	Eat. Sleep. Wash.
Dritan knows when to eat, sleep and wash	

himself. His parents
taught him that.

> Repeat. Repeat. Repeat.

They have no interest in
him.

> It's hard when you don't
> speak their
> language.

At night, Dritan
sometimes cries.
Not loudly.

> We can hear him.
> We can't hug him.
> There are procedures.

Dritan is just a little kid.

> Procedures keep children
> safe.
> And a hug isn't safe.

They have no interest in the other boy

who lives here.

GARETH I'm Gareth and I fucking hate you.

CHORUS Gareth isn't very well in the head, Dritan thinks. (**GARETH** *sticks his fingers up his bottom and waves them in* **DRITAN**'s *face*) Dritan wants to ask him "Why would you do that? That's mad. And disgusting." He wants to tell Geoffrey and Anne, but he hasn't got the words. And then one night...

DRITAN *goes to get into bed. The sheets are brown with* **GARETH**'s *excrement.*

DRITAN *pins* **GARETH** *and puts the excrement in his mouth.*

Dritan tells Gareth, "Eat it, you bastard." He is screaming and shouting it over and over but –

GEOFFREY What are you doing to him? Get off him. Dritan!

GEOFFREY *and* ANNE *pull* DRITAN *off* GARETH.

CHORUS Gareth puts shit in Dritan's bed but it's Dritan who gets the shit for it. Loads of shit. Because he can't explain to them that it's Gareth's shit and not his and what he did with it. So, they think it's his fault.

But they don't send him away.

He wants them to.

DRITAN *on his mobile phone.*

DRITAN Alfred, this place is miles from you. Which is probably why social services want me here right? So, you can't get to me?

ALFRED Calm down, little man. What's the address?

DRITAN I don't know.

ALFRED Aren't there any letters? Any bills lying around? Find a letter and phone me back with the address and postcode. I'll be there.

DRITAN When? Come now.

ALFRED *arrives.*

ALFRED Okay, so I think I am on the right street.

DRITAN Wait, I'll come outside.

ANNE Where are you going, Dritan...? Dritan? I asked you a question. You aren't allowed to go outside without...

DRITAN Alf, I can see you, I'm waving to you.

ALFRED *and* DRITAN *hug.*

ANNE *(to* ALFRED*)* Oh my – you're the brother then. Geoffrey! The brother is here. *(To* ALFRED*)* You're not supposed to be here. You aren't allowed to see him.

DRITAN What are you talking about this is my brother.

ALFRED I've just come to see if he is okay.

ANNE You're not taking him.

ALFRED I'm not going to take him.

ANNE Geoffrey...! *(To* **ALFRED***)* You heard me. He has to stay here. You can't have him. He's been removed from your care. You need to leave now please, or we're calling the police.

ALFRED Why? I just want to see that the little man is doing okay. And to give him this. *(He hands* **DRITAN** *a gift)*

ANNE Call the police, Geoffrey.

ALFRED Tan, I have to go. But I will come back. I promise. I won't leave you, okay?

DRITAN But I want you to see you. I want you. Alfred.

ANNE Come inside, Dritan... Dritan.

> **ALFRED** *leaves.*

CHORUS Why do Geoffrey and Anne think Alfred is dangerous? Dritan doesn't understand.

> **DRITAN** *opens* **ALFRED***'s gift: it's a new mobile phone.*

SOCIAL WORKER/INTERPRETER *(not in unison)* These cost five hundred quid, apparently.

CHORUS Dritan reads the social worker's energy as she speaks to him.

SOCIAL WORKER We know what's going on, Dritan, we know.

CHORUS She doesn't know. She doesn't have a clue.

SOCIAL WORKER/INTERPETER *(not in unison)* What does Alfred do, exactly?

How can you make that much money working in a car wash?

Boys his age don't earn that sort of money legally.

CHORUS Dritan tells his interpreter to tell them he says, "Fuck you. You know nothing."

But he can tell by the looks on the social workers' faces that he isn't translating properly.

SOCIAL WORKER/INTERPRETER *(not in unison)* We do know. It's our job to know.

DRITAN You think Alfred is in some sort of criminal gang. My brother works in a car wash really fucking hard seven days a week. He earns all his money cos British people have a lot of fucking dirty cars, alright?

CHORUS But he hasn't got these words in English to explain it to them and no one is listening anyway.

A school bell rings.

CHORUS Dritan is put into school. Into year six. He should be in year seven or eight. But it's because he can't speak English. And all these kids are younger, and they are really welcoming...

SCHOOL KIDS	CHORUS
– Are you a Paki?	
	What's a Paki?
– Are you Saddam Hussein?	
	Dritan knows what that means.
– Are you Muslim?	

CHORUS Dritan wonders why none of the teachers do anything. He knows they sometimes overhear.

SCHOOL KIDS – He's a fucking towel head.

– Are you a Taliban?

– He is fucking Taliban.

– Osama.

– Osama bin Laden.

– Osama.

DRITAN *looks at them and eats their hearts. The* SCHOOL
KIDS *back off. But they come back. They spit, they shove,
they hit.* DRITAN *fights.*

GEOFFREY I can't believe you got excluded in the first week,
Dritan. You can't fight in school here, do you understand.
If you keep fighting, they'll have to remove you from the
school, remove you from us. Now you just sit here on your
bed and think about that. No watching *Countdown* for you
today. No TV for a week. No sweets for a week.

CHORUS	DRITAN
Dritan hates	
Fucking Countdown.	Fucking Countdown.
He hates	
Fucking Geoffrey and Anne.	Fucking Geoffrey and Anne.
He hates	
This fucking country.	This fucking country,
	man... It's nuts.

CHORUS Dritan thinks that what British people don't seem to
understand is that no one really wants to come here. They
think they do because they have to get out of where they
are. But when they get here, this is what they have to live.

He wants his brother but the system won't give him back.

It won't give him back to Alfred.

It won't give him back to his mum and dad.

Dritan wonders why these people are called "carers".

They say it's their job to care.

Foster caring ain't no job.

Don't call this caring.

Geoffrey and Anne don't beat him, they don't rape him.

It's not what they do to him is wrong.

It's more what they don't do.

DRITAN *is all by himself. He cries.* GEOFFREY *and* ANNE
see this. No one comforts him.

Forward forward forward

Or down

Or nothing.

19. Learning to Swim (Again)

CHORUS In school everyone thinks Dritan is stupid or slow or something. Because he can't speak any English, so he is in the lowest classes for everything. But Dritan can do maths.

DRITAN I'm in the highest class for this.

CHORUS And the teacher sees this. When she sets him a problem –

DRITAN I'm just – whoosh.

CHORUS Back home he was just average. Here, they think he's a maths genius. So Dritan starts learning English.

And the first English words he learns are:

DRITAN Shit... Fuck you... Prick.

DRITAN fights.

CHORUS So, the more English he learns, the more fights he gets into.

DRITAN But now I have one friend.

In the dinner queue at school...

DAVE I'm Dave. Pleased to meet you. And you are Drit-an, okay? Now then, I noticed you wondering what to get for lunch. Don't eat the shepherd's pie. It's probably got rat in it. Have the sausage roll and beans instead. Sau-sage roll. Okay?

DINNER LADY What you having, boys?

DAVE Oh, he doesn't understand English. Wait a minute, I'll translate. She says, "Wh-at y-ou ha-ving?" Okay?

DINNER LADY I could have done that translation myself, David.

DAVE He'll have sausage roll and beans, please, Diane, thank you.

DRITAN He thinks he is looking after me. But I'm really looking after him.

CHORUS Dritan sticks up for him because he is his only friend. Cos Dave gets bullied too.

DRITAN *fights.*

20. Respite in heaven

CHORUS Geoffrey and Anne are going on holiday.

DRITAN But I'm not going on holiday with them. Because they need a rest from me.

CHORUS So, Dritan's moving again.

DRITAN To somewhere called "Respite".

GILLIAN Hi, Dritan. Is that how I should say your name...?

DRITAN Yes. That's right.

GILLIAN I'm Gillian and this is my husband, John, these are the boys: Jack, Sam and Jamie.

BOYS – You wanna play football?

– You wanna play Spiderman?

– You wanna play my PlayStation?

– You wanna watch James Bond?

– Dritan, come and do this.

– Dritan, hey, over here.

– Dritan, hey.

– Hey.

– Hey.

– Hey.

CHORUS It's just like having little brothers. They just let him be in their family. Like a real part of their family. When it comes to dinner time...

JOHN Right, lads, we're having takeaway. Me and your mum are having pizza, what you boys having?

BOYS – Pizza.

– Pizza.

– Kebab.

JOHN Dritan? What you having?

DRITAN Kebab. Please.

CHORUS These foster parents are really like actual parents. Not his own but like them. Dritan can/ help himself –

GILLIAN Help yourself to anything you like from the kitchen when you're hungry. If you don't stretch you starve. Alright, darling?

CHORUS He has his own bed which no one puts any shit in. And this Foster Dad is cool.

He plays music. Music: "ROCKSTAR" by Nickelback*.

JOHN *(sings)*
HEY ... HEY ... I WANNA BE A ROCKSTAR.

DRITAN/CHORUS And they wanna know things about me. They ask me actual questions about me.

PARENTS AND BOYS – Where do you come from?

– What's it like?

– What does your brother do?

– Do you like music?

– Who's your favourite football team?

– What do your mum and dad do?

CHORUS And Dritan tries to answer in the best English he's got.

DRITAN/CHORUS And they listen to me.

CHORUS No one in this country's ever listened to him before. But John and Gillian from Gillingham do. And in this house, like his own home, everyone does everything together. Even the grown-ups.

They play games, go to the park. Climb trees.

---

* A licence to produce HOW NOT TO DROWN does not include a performance licence for "ROCKSTAR". For further information, please see Music Use Note on page v.

DRITAN/CHORUS This. Is. Like. Heaven... I don't get into no fights here. Not one. For two whole weeks.

GILLIAN So, do you like it here, Dritan?

DRITAN/CHORUS Yeah. I do.

GILLIAN Good. That's good. Cos we like having you here. It's like you're just one of us... Would you like to come back again and stay for a bit longer?

DRITAN Please.

GILLIAN Maybe stay for good?

DRITAN/CHORUS Yes, please.

CHORUS Dritan really, really want this to happen, to stay with John and Gillian from Gillingham. And he just knows that if Alfred turned up here, they'd never call the police. They'd invite him right into their house.

But, two weeks later...

Back at **GEOFFREY** *and* **ANNE***'s.*

ANNE We brought you a T-shirt from Butlins, Dritan... Oh it's a bit small isn't it? Have you put on weight? What were they feeding you? Did you have a nice time, Dritan?

(**DRITAN** *nods*) Well, you really must have... They wanted to keep you. For good. Asked social work and everything.

DRITAN	**CHORUS**
Did they?	Did they really?
	They really did.

GEOFFREY Totally inappropriate. They should never have promised you that.

DRITAN They didn't. / They just –

ANNE Totally inexcusable. They're just respite carers. They know that. It's not allowed. They know that. Anyway, social work said no.

GEOFFREY Quite rightly.

ANNE But you're safe with us.

GEOFFREY Oh. By the way, Gareth isn't coming back to live here again. They've found him somewhere more suitable.

CHORUS Social work have found Gareth somewhere more suitable? What about him? He really found somewhere. Somewhere people actually want him to be. Like a proper home. But the system has procedures.

21. Foster Care #4

PRISCILLA Hi Dritan, I'm Pricilla, your new social worker.

DRITAN/CHORUS Until Priscilla. She's not like any other social worker I've ever met before. For a start she's from South Africa. And she actually visits me all the times she's supposed to.

PRISCILLA Actually, Anne and Geoffrey, I think I'd rather speak to Dritan alone, if you don't mind. He has a right to a private conversation with me, so if you wouldn't mind giving us the space, please?

ANNE Oh... I see... Well, I suppose so. I can put *Countdown* on in the kitchen. Come on, Geoff.

PRISCILLA Thank you. *(To DRITAN)* Now, then. How do you think it's going here?

DRITAN I want to see my brother. I don't know why you won't let me see him by myself. He's not mafia. He's not a fucking criminal. Don't you see how racist you are all being?

PRISCILLA ...Yes... I can see that you would think that was racist. Maybe it is.

CHORUS She really listens. She takes notes. She isn't faking it. Dritan can tell. Energy.

PRISCILLA So, you want me to find you somewhere better to live?

CHORUS Dritan is twelve, nearly thirteen years old and he is moving again. But now he's even further away from Alfred. From this new place, it takes two hours to get to Ilford by public transport.

BRIAN Brian.

MARY Mary.

ALEX And I'm Alex.

DRITAN/CHORUS Alex is an older, Albanian kid. And he's okay. And there is just us here – no other kids. So, I ask him:

DRITAN What about these foster carers, are they alright? Cos I don't want to be nowhere worse than before, bruv.

ALEX Yeah, they're fine. They don't hassle you. It's easy.

CHORUS And they do seem alright. Brian is into his motor bikes. He has loads of cars and engines and jet skis. Brian teaches him how to ride them.

DRITAN/CHORUS Brian is a cool guy.

I think he likes me.

I know she likes me. But him...

I can't read this dude...

DRITAN *calls* **ALFRED.**

DRITAN *(on phone)* Alfred, when can I come stay with you for good? You're old enough now. You can look after me.

ALFRED Look, Dritan. I want you to be with me. I've tried, but the social workers aren't going to let you. Not yet. If you want to make something of your life then stay in foster care. Stay in school. Think about it.

DRITAN/CHORUS I do think about it.

And these new carers do seem okay, like Alex says...

School.

HEAD TEACHER So, Dritan and Foster Dad. Thanks for coming to this return to school meeting. Now, I hope four days at home has drilled into you the seriousness of what you did last week and that violence will not be tolerated in this school. What do you say?

DRITAN ...

HEAD TEACHER You don't seem very repentant. What do you say Foster Dad?

BRIAN My name's Brian... Dritan understands he was violent. But does the school understand what triggered the fight? A boy called him a racist name / and Dritan felt he had to...

HEAD TEACHER And the boy has been spoken to and I can assure you he will not do it again. But can Dritan assure me, can Foster Dad assure me that he won't be violent again?

DRITAN If someone pushes me I'm gonna push back, okay?

HEAD TEACHER If you can't assure me of better behaviour in future, then I can't let you back into this school. I'll send you home for another week. Unless you apologise to the boy in question.

DRITAN No fucking way.

HEAD TEACHER Watch your language when you are talking to me, Mr Kastrati. I am sure Foster Dad will agree with me that this behaviour, this attitude is unacceptable and will have to stop. What do you say, Foster Dad?

BRIAN Brian... I say... Well, actually, no I don't really agree with you. I think Dritan was the victim here. Of racial abuse. And he was just defending himself. And I think the school should be doing more to protect his rights and not those of the bullies, actually. So, no, he won't be apologising, and if that doesn't suit you, we'll see you in another week.

DRITAN/CHORUS I think I'll give this dude a chance. Maybe he really does care. I'll try to make a bond with him anyway.

I really try.

He is nice to me. I am giving him a little bit of myself. A little trust. He is nice to me. But...

I can't talk about anything I feel. If I do say something about how I feel, he says:

BRIAN Oh. Okay, then.

DRITAN/CHORUS That's it. Just:

BRIAN Oh. Okay, then.

DRITAN/CHORUS	**BRIAN**
What is that about?	
	They're tough these kids.

I want to give him part of
me.

They've seen a lot. A lot
has happened to them,
stuff we can't
even imagine, I expect.

But
This is just a job to him,
isn't it?

I see the way he looks at
me.

I can't give him even a
little bit of me.

Does he really need us?
He doesn't need us. Not
really.

It's not what he and Mary
do to me. It's what
they don't do.

He's a survivor.
Maybe sometimes he
needs a hug. But...

A hug isn't safe.

I can't live with my
brother, legally.
I can't go back home until
I am sixteen.
But until then, I just have
to...
Cos...
Forward forward forward
Or down
Or nothing.

SCHOOL KIDS – Are you a Paki?

– Are you Saddam Hussein?

– Are you Muslim?

– He is a fucking towel head.

– Are you a Taliban?

– He is fucking Taliban.

– Osama.

DRITAN *fights.*

22. Michael Tulloch

TULLOCH Alright settle down now guys, settle down. My name is...

DRITAN/CHORUS Mr Tulloch.

TULLOCH Michael Tulloch.

DRITAN/CHORUS This new teacher comes when I am in year nine.

TULLOCH And I am here to teach you drama. When people hear my name they're expecting a white guy. But, hello, I'm a big black guy.

DRITAN Big dude. West Indian. Dreadlocks. I'd never met anyone like Tulloch.

TULLOCH So, let me tell you a little bit about me. I'm English. My parents are from Jamaica, but I was born here in England. So that makes me English, right...? Not for some people. For some people I'm not English. When I was growing up, I'd see signs in the shop windows and hotels near where I lived, and do you know what they said? "No blacks, no dogs, no Irish."

DRITAN/CHORUS The bad kids, like me, we'd never listen to teachers. But this guy...

Tulloch really saw me. One time though, I really pissed him off. This Albanian kid and me were going at it in class. And I got sent to the corridor. Again. So I waited for him and when the bell rang:

DRITAN *attacks the boy. Fight.*

TULLOCH Break it up.

What do you think you are doing, fighting each other?

(to **DRITAN***)* You fucking idiot. You two should not be fighting each other. You should not be fighting him, of all people,

do you get me? (**DRITAN** *nods*) Good. Good, now would you like to get to class, please?

DRITAN/CHORUS He died a few years ago. And at his funeral no one wore black. It was a big celebration with all the food and music and life he loved.

Without Michael Tulloch, I wouldn't be the me I am today.

He made me feel...safe.

I didn't need to fight anymore.

23. The End of Foster Care

DRITAN *comes home from school. He knocks.*

DRITAN/CHORUS Brian!

Mary!

No one answers. He sits in the garden and waits. It rains.

Why won't they give me a key?

It's been three years since I came to these carers.

Three years, the longest I have lived anywhere since I came to this country.

BRIAN *and* **MARY** *enter.*

I am feeling...something...for you.

In my country, we say, "if you live with the pig, you learn to love the pig".

But I still don't have a key to this house.

Alex has left and is in his own flat.

Dritan is starting to care.

And I hope that the more they see me care, the more they will...

But... The more he likes them

The less I feel they like me.

Just give me a key.

Alright, it's not really about having a key, it's...

It's been a long time since...

Say it.

I can't say it.

It's been a long time since he felt really...

Loved.

DRITAN *(to* **BRIAN***)* Brian, I'm not staying here after I am sixteen.

BRIAN Why not?

DRITAN I'm just not staying.

BRIAN But it's going good here, yes.

DRITAN It's alright.

BRIAN Well, why don't you stay then...? Look sit down and talk to me for a second. Sit down. Look, you know we have a good relationship, right...? You don't make any trouble for us and we don't make trouble for you, yes...? We're happy to have you here until you are eighteen.

Okay, Dritan, let's just be really straight up with each other: this is a good business arrangement, isn't it? It works for both of us. Anyone else they give us, it mightn't work so well. If you stay with us until you're eighteen, I'll make you a deal, okay? Stay til then and when you move out on your eighteenth birthday I'll give you three grand. How about that?

DRITAN/CHORUS Did he just offer me money?

BRIAN There's a deal for you, right there.

DRITAN He offered me money.

BRIAN And it can go towards your Uni fees, or whatever you like.

DRITAN/CHORUS I don't want your money. I want...

BRIAN What do you say?

DRITAN/CHORUS And I want you to want me.

Dritan thinks...

Maybe when it's your job to care you can't really care that much, not really.

But do you know what that feels like for a little kid or a teenager?

I'll tell you what foster care feels like: like living always in a hotel.

Yes, you have a bed, someone does your washing, feeds you, cleans your room.

And the staff smile at you. Cos they're paid to do it.

It's nice maybe for a few days, a few weeks. But you need more to really live a life than that.

You need something which feels like yours.

Somewhere you belong.

Somewhere like home.

And you can't fake "home" if you're a foster carer. You have to be "home".

BRIAN Come on, you know it makes financial sense for all of us.

DRITAN/CHORUS Dritan thinks...

Fuck you. I was right. I read you right... Fuck your money.

On my sixteenth birthday, I move out. Into Alex's flat with him. Good old Alex, I can always rely on him. This is it. The end of hotel foster care.

DRITAN I move into Alex's spare room.

ALEX You want to go home, right? Unpack your stuff. I'll book the plane tickets. Don't worry, you can pay me back whenever.

24. Going Home

On the aeroplane.

DRITAN/CHORUS I am on a plane to Tirana. My parents moved there a few years ago. And anyway, because of my asylum my UK travel document doesn't allow me to go back to Kosova. The flight takes just a few hours, but it is five years since I saw my parents. But I am going to my real mum and dad, to my own culture, my own language. I think I am going home.

At the baggage carousel.

At baggage reclaim, the Vodafone poster on the wall says, "Power to you" in Albanian. Yes. I must be home.

I've called my parents and they are going to meet me.

Will they recognise me?

Will I recognise them?

DAD Hey, you! Come here!

DRITAN/CHORUS They look the same. But older.

MUM Dritan... You're so big now.

> **MUM** *bursts into tears. She hugs him.*

DAD Alright, let him go. Let the boy get his bearings. And let's get him home. Come on, get into the car.

DRITAN/CHORUS We get in the car and my dad is driving down all these dirt roads. I don't know where.

"Dad, why are you going this way?

CHORUS But Dritan's dad doesn't understand him.

Because Dritan doesn't have all the proper words anymore, in Albanian.

And so he speaks some in English because English is the language he speaks now.

He can't talk to them.

Tell them.

He wants to tell them so many things.

They arrive at his parents' house.

He doesn't recognise anything. It's their home. Not his.

Dritan needs to go home.

Go north.

To Luli.

He gets a taxi over the border into Kosova.

Screw his UK travel document, he needs to see her.

On the way, he stops, just for a few minutes in his old village.

It's a ghost town.

Only three or four blocks of flats are left standing but derelict.

And one of them is where his home was.

Dritan stands and look at it. He looks at the river, the waterfall...

Small... Everything is so small...

And grey. It used to be so green here.

DRITAN Nothing is like I remember it. I could go into my old flat, the building is open. But, no... I don't want to kill my home in my memory...

CHORUS There is nothing to go back to here...

In Luli's town everything is new and shiny and clean. Everything has been rebuilt. There must be loads of money here. Maybe because of the gold...

Dritan doesn't know her address exactly. She just told me to come to a certain shop and ask where the old tree used to be. It doesn't exist anymore but everyone knows where it used to be.

DRITAN Fucking hell, this is weird. People in England have addresses...what if I get lost?

LULI Tan, come here.

  LULI *hugs him.*

CHORUS Luli... Now this feels right.

LULI Are you hungry? What do you want to eat? I thought I would make you sejouk.

DRITAN/CHORUS What's that?

LULI It used to be your favourite. You'll like it... Come on. I want you to meet someone.

CHORUS And Dritan meets his nephew for this first time. He's three years old. And that's...a bit like...uh...

DRITAN A slap in the face... Y'know – family. I've never seen... I have missed so much.

CHORUS And his nephew is looking at him as if to say, "Who are you?"

DRITAN I have missed so much.

CHORUS And everyone says that he looks like Dritan. And Dritan lifts him up and Luli takes a picture.

DRITAN That's the first picture I ever put on my Facebook page.

LULI Here it is – sejouk.

DRITAN As soon as she takes it out of the oven and I smell the smell and suddenly – oooh. Yes, I know what this is. And the taste... Ah...

CHORUS He feels at home here with Luli. And it's only when he is leaving that it hits him...

DRITAN I don't want to leave. I don't want to leave this feeling behind. I am only just used to being here...to being home... to having family.

CHORUS He hasn't had a family for five years. For five years every time he started missing home he had to lock that feeling out. To save himself.

DRITAN But now I am at home.

CHORUS And then he goes back to his parents.

But it is very hard to be there because although he knows they are his parents, he has forgotten what they feel like. What having them feels like inside himself.

It's mad.

He phones Alfred, his brother, who is back in England.

DRITAN I'm back at dad and m- m- m-

CHORUS Just say it. What is wrong with you?

DRITAN I'm at m- m- m-

CHORUS He can't say the word "mum". In English. Because he hasn't ever had a "mum" in English.

Other people had a mum. But in English that word has never been his. So he switches and says it in Albanian.

DRITAN "Marmi".

CHORUS With his parents it is still not like home.

DRITAN It's like I had forced myself to forget and now I can't remember what it's like to just relax and be with them. Why did my dad do this to me? I was eleven years old...

CHORUS One day, he asks him.

DAD Well, everyone was leaving after the war. The situation was unstable. There was no future for you here.

DRITAN Yes, I know about the political situation. But that doesn't answer my question. Why did you personally send me personally away like that?

DAD There were so many guns floating around because of the war. No jobs. Just mafia. And people seeking revenge.

DRITAN What revenge? What are you talking about?

DAD Okay, I rushed. But the window of opportunity was closing. The British were shutting down their borders, we didn't have time to wait. If I'd waited... I had to get you out of there.

DRITAN I was eleven years old. Just a little kid. How could you do that? I want to know. I want to understand why.

DAD Because of this. Exactly this. Because... You. You are relentless.

DRITAN But you don't really know me, do you? You know the eleven-year-old boy but not the man. You don't know what I went through.

DAD So what would you rather have, then? Tell me. To have the life, the opportunities, the education you've had in England, or to end up dead before you were eighteen? Which...?

DRITAN I was just a little kid.

Pause. They both look at an image of the younger DRITAN.

DRITAN If you could go back and do it all again, would you make the same choice?

DAD No fucking way.

26. Home?

DRITAN/CHORUS I've been in Albania for two weeks. I'm standing in the immigration queue and the border guard who is stamping my travel document says

IMMIGRATION OFFICER Why were you in the country? You're an immigrant.

DRITAN I'm what...? What...? I'm not a fucking immigrant.

IMMIGRATION OFFICER You are not from here. So answer, why were you visiting Albania?

CHORUS Dritan thought that there were no borders between the Albanian people.

DRITAN I was visiting my parents.

IMMIGRATION OFFICER But your UK travel document says you're from Yugoslavia. So, why are you here? Look, if you don't answer me, then I have to detain you.

AIRPORT ANNOUNCEMENT This is the last final call for all last remaining passengers travelling on the Alitalia flight 6546 please proceed to departure gate three where your flight is already boarding. That's last remaining passengers please proceed to gate three immediately.

DRITAN/CHORUS Do I want to go home? I mean, England... I don't know... Where is my home? It's not here. And it's not there... It is here but... My language isn't my language. And my parents...

Are definitely my parents.

I just need to remember.

I just have to learn everything all over again.

Forward forward forward

Or down

Or nothing.

End

Dritan and his nephew, in Kosova, 2006.

VISIT THE SAMUEL FRENCH BOOKSHOP AT THE ROYAL COURT THEATRE

Browse plays and theatre books, get expert advice and enjoy a coffee

Samuel French Bookshop
Royal Court Theatre
Sloane Square
London
SW1W 8AS
020 7565 5024

Shop from thousands of titles on our website

 samuelfrench.co.uk

 samuelfrenchltd

 samuel french uk